FOUNDATIONAL LEGAL ISSUES FOR PRE-SERVICE TEACHERS

Henry S. Williams

Central Washington University

KENDALL/HUNT PUBLISHING COMPANY
4050 Westmark Drive   Dubuque, Iowa 52002

Cover image © Digital Juice.

Contents

CHAPTER 1

Introduction   1
Sources Available to Teachers' Legal Status   2
History in a Nutshell   2
Racial Segregation in the U.S.   4
Federal Court System   13

CHAPTER 2

The United States Constitution   17
Amendments   17
The Legal Procedures   19
The Constitution and Schools   21
Prayer in School   22
The Free Exercise Clause   26
Free Speech in School   29
Free Speech and Teachers   34
Case Studies   35

CHAPTER 3

Due Process   39
The Elements of Substantive Due Process   42
FERPA—General Guideline for Students   44
Peer Grading   46
School Discipline   47
Corporal Punishment in School   48
Suspension: In School and Out-of-School   51

Exclusion from Extracurricular Activities   53
Zero Tolerance   54
Case Studies on Zero Tolerance   55
Drug Testing   57
Case One   59
Case Two   60

CHAPTER 4

Teacher-Board Relations and Certification   65
Academic Freedom   66
Some Relevant Court Decisions on Academic Freedom   69
Teacher Evaluation   73

CHAPTER 5

Search and Seizure   75
Guideline for Search   81
Case Studies on Search   82

CHAPTER 6

Child Abuse   85
Child Abuse and Neglect   86
Definition of Child Abuse   86
Abuse of Children by Parents   87
Abuse of Children by Teachers   88
Child Abuse Facts   89
Indicators of Abused Children   89
The Role of the School   90
Grooming   92
Common Sense Rules on Touching   92

CHAPTER 7

Tort Liability   95

GLOSSARY   105

REFERENCES   115

Acknowledgments

▼

Of the many persons who provided me with support in this project, some deserve to be mentioned. Osman Alawiye, a friend and colleague at Central Washington University for his legal technical support, the students for their contribution to the development and critique of this project, Tina Clark and Tami Swain, Central Washington University, for their editorial work. Special thanks to Leif Hanson for his contribution to the section on segregation in America, and Darrel Harris on academic freedom.

Infinite thanks to my dear wife and friend, Peggy Williams, for her unconditional support throughout my endeavor to complete this project.

Chapter

INTRODUCTION

Since a number of legal questions arise in the day-to-day running of schools, a school teacher needs to have some understanding of school law that will enhance better classroom practices and also a foundational knowledge of the Constitution. According to Harold J. Berman and William R. Greiner, "In an elementary and concrete sense, an understanding of the nature and functions of law is essential to a proper understanding of many other disciplines. A student of economics or business administration, for example, must be somewhat at a loss to understand what cooperation is, or what property means, or how a collective bargaining agreement works, without any background in the legal system (p. 8)." Teachers need to know under what conditions they may be liable for students' injuries, what legal authority the teacher has in controlling the conduct of pupils, what the teacher's rights are and what the rights are of the students, and what the sources are of legal control over schools. A student in teacher education can *profitably* study legal reasoning and processes in order to update ideas about child abuse and other issues affecting education.

Knowledge of school law is important to the teacher just as the law is important to all citizens. Educational leaders need to know the law for reasons beyond being able to defend themselves and exercise their rights. One of the fundamental principles of our jobs is to produce students who are law-abiding citizens. To be able to carry out the daily tasks that are assigned to us as teachers, we should certainly attempt to observe the laws underlying our democratic society and should not knowingly or through ignorance flaunt the basic intent of the laws.

Finally, classroom teachers are asked to study school law not only for the sake of understanding the foundations of social order, but for the sake of social values, including the constitutional rights of the individuals they work with.

SOURCES AVAILABLE TO TEACHERS' LEGAL STATUS

Court decisions are a major source of information available to teachers. Teachers should be cognizant of the decisions that constitute an important source of law. These decisions are available in university or local law libraries. Public laws are another information source; for example, since the 1950s Congress has been very active in the passage of laws governing the civil rights of students, teachers, and the disabled. State policies are a third source of information.

One source of policies available to teachers are those of the local boards of education. Their policies have the same effect as laws because the boards represent an arm of our individual state governments.

HISTORY IN A NUTSHELL

Twenty-two years after the landing of the Mayflower at Plymouth and six years after the founding of Harvard College, the general court of the Massachusetts Bay Colony, meeting in Boston in 1642, enacted what is probably the first school law to be passed in what would become the United States.

The law said, in part, that: "Ye chosen men appointed for managing the prudential affairs of the same shall henceforth stand charged with the care of the redress of this evil... the "evil" being that great neglect of many parents and masters in training up their children in learning and labor, and other implements which may be profitable to the common wealth...." Town councils were given the responsibility of all "parents and masters," and "their children," concerning their calling and "implement" especially their reading and understanding of the principles of religion "and the capital laws of the country." Fines were assessed on those parents and masters who refused, when required, to render suitable account to the town council. The significance of this law was that it established a new legal principle toward education: the education of children was deemed to be a proper subject for legal control.

In order to make the 1642 law effective, the Massachusetts Bay Colony passed the "Olde Deluder Satan Act" in 1647. This act corrected an oversight in the act of 1642: nowhere in the previous act was specific provision made for the actual establishment of schools by the town councils. Hence, "being one chief project of that old deluder, Satan, to keep men from the knowledge of the scriptures... (by) keeping them in an unknown tongue... The act of 1647 therefore orders that every township in this jurisdiction, after the Lord hath increased you to 50 householders, shall then and thenceforth appoint one of your numbers to teach all such children as shall resort to him to read and write." In towns which had increased to 100 householders, the law directed that a grammar school be set up to instruct youth for the university. The wages of the teachers were to be paid by the parents and masters of the children or inhabitants of the town in general "by way of supply." This is the first known legal reference to the support of schools by public taxation in this country.

The first public high school was established in Boston in 1821. Massachusetts law, in 1827, provided that every town having 500 families or more must establish a high school. United States history, algebra, bookkeeping, geometry, and surveying were offered. Each town having 4,000 or more inhabitants was required to include the study of Greek, Latin, history, rhetoric, and logic. A penalty was issued to towns that refused or neglected to provide a high school. The 1827 Massachusetts act was mandatory. Many other states passed permissive regulations enabling towns to start high schools if they wished to do so.

These permissive regulations were met with challenges, the most famous being the Kalamazoo Case in 1872. Objection was brought by a Mr. Stuart, a Michigan taxpayer, on the grounds that paying taxes for the support of a high school and the employment of a superintendent of schools violated the Michigan constitution. While not contesting the power of the state to tax for common schools, Stuart maintained that the high school was not necessarily a part of the state public school system and that education beyond the common school level was a luxury to be paid for privately. The Supreme Court of Michigan held otherwise.

After noting with approval that the state had provided not only for common schools but also for a state university, the court pointed out that failure to provide secondary education would be inconsistent and improvident. To the argument that classical and foreign languages were the accomplishment of the few, the court expressed surprise that anyone would question the right of the state to bring a liberal education within reach of youth of all classes within the state.

The Kalamazoo Case had an immediate effect on the growth of public high schools all over the country, especially where boards of education had hesitated to set up high schools due to their view of their ambiguous legal position to do so.

Racial Segregation in the U.S.

Today we live in a society where many people find it impossible to imagine a school with only white students and teachers. Our public schools now consist of a variety of students from different backgrounds. Most public schools pride themselves in being diverse. However, public schools have not always been what they are today. Fifty years ago, most school districts refused to allow African Americans to attend the same schools as whites. This was the same was for Asians and Latino Americans. African Americans and their supporters fought hard to overcome the doctrine of "separate but equal" which led to the Civil Rights Act of 1964.

The concept of Civil Rights is dismissed as unnecessary by those who need not benefit from it. But, for those in the path of inequality, it is a concept impossible to ignore. When racial discrimination is accepted by the majority of people, reversing its effects has proven to be an arduous process. It is one that, as a whole, the American people have yet to complete. Still, there is hope. There remains one resource as yet untapped by this nation: the past. An intensive look into the past can put light on what has been, in many ways, a dark and painful birth for equality.

In 1863, President Lincoln submitted the Emancipation Proclamation, to free black slaves in America. This helped bring about the Civil War because white farmers in the south relied on their slaves for free labor. Soon after, the Civil War congress passed the Thirteenth Amendment that freed slaves regardless of their home state. These progressive steps were a beginning; however, alone they would not suffice to bring about equality. Blacks were now stuck in the south with dangerously hostile whites (Hartin, 2003).

Reconstruction, which lasted from 1866 to 1877, was congress' attempt to find a proper place for blacks in the north and the south. Congress knew it had to reorganize the southern states, integrate them back into the union, and find a way for blacks and whites to live together peacefully. As a result of this effort there was a dramatic increase in the number of black students who attended public schools. These newly freed slaves were hungry to learn in the same way as the white students. This was also the time that Congress passed the Civil Rights Acts, which guaranteed that all people would have the same access to public accommodation. However, many states chose to ignore these new laws and continue to practice racial discrimination (Nolen, 2003).

After the Reconstruction, bitter whites in the south enacted a series of new "Jim Crow" laws that legitimized the idea of separation among whites and blacks in schools and other public forums. The idea of "separate but equal" was born. During this time there were constant efforts by Congress to help the black community realize their rights under the law. There were also efforts from organizations like the Ku Klux Klan to keep blacks and whites separate, on all accounts (Nolen, 2003).

One of the most important cases to uphold separation of blacks and whites was the *Plessy v. Ferguson* case of 1892. Louisiana law required blacks and whites to sit in separate compartments on passenger trains, and failure to do so was punishable by a twenty-five dollar fine or twenty days in jail. A 30-year-old man named Homer Plessy, who was seven-eighths white and one-eighth black, sat in the "whites only" section of the East Louisiana Railroad. He was found guilty and promptly jailed. In his defense, Plessy believed that the separate car law was a violation of the Thirteenth and Fourteenth Amendments of the United States Constitution. The judge in this case, Justice Ferguson, declared that since the train stayed within the state of Louisiana it could have separate cars for blacks and whites if it so desired. Thus, Plessy was found guilty of sitting in the "white" car (Hartin, 2003).

Homer Plessy appealed the court findings in Louisiana's Supreme Court, only to have the Louisiana Supreme Court sustain the findings from the previous decision. Plessy decided to appeal to the Supreme Court of the United States. The court reviewed the case and ultimately found Plessy guilty. Henry Brown, the justice who spoke for the eight-justice majority stated:

> The Separate Car Act does not conflict with the Thirteenth Amendment, which abolished slavery...[it] is too clear for argument... A statute which implies merely a legal distinction between the white and colored races—a distinction which is founded in the color of the two races, which must always exist, so long as white men are distinguished from the other race by color—has no tendency to destroy the legal equality of the two races...The object of the Fourteenth Amendment was undoubtedly to enforce the absolute equality of the two races before the law, but in the same nature of things it could not have been intended to abolish distinctions based upon color, or to enforce social, as distinguished from political equality, or a commingling of the two races upon terms unsatisfactory to either (Hartin, 2003).

This kind of rhetoric from a United States Supreme Court justice makes it amazing that this nation has made any progress at all. One justice did have the foresight to see beyond color and look at the case with justice and equality in mind. John Harlan had this to say after the decision:

Our constitution is color-blind, and neither knows nor tolerates classes among citizens. In respect of civil rights, all citizens are equal before the law…In my opinion, the judgment this day will, in time, prove to be quite as pernicious as the decision made by this tribunal in the Dred Scott case…The present decision, it may well be apprehended, will not only stimulate aggressions, more or less brutal and irritating, upon the admitted rights of colored citizens, but will encourage the belief that it is possible, by means of state enactments, to adopt the recent amendments to the Constitution (Hartin, 2003).

This case was devastating to the cause of equality and justice for all citizens. There was now a court precedent that gave states the go-ahead to enact laws that segregated classes based on skin color. Segregation in this country would continue to thrive until the landmark case of *Brown v. Board of Education* in 1954.

It is important to acknowledge the fact that life in our country was still not equal for all people. There were many improvements made during the closing stages of the nineteenth century, but there were also many steps backward. For 50 years after *Plessy v. Ferguson,* segregation was the status quo in the United States. It was not until *Brown v. Board of Education* that things took a turn for the better. 1954 was the year, Topeka, Kansas was the site, and the lives of thousands of minorities were at risk. Linda Brown was prevented from attending a white school nearby rather than an elementary school which was further away because of her race. This case challenged the case of *Plessy v. Ferguson* and its ruling in favor of segregation. Black community leaders took action against segregated schools. Aided by the local chapter of the National Association for the Advancement of Colored People (NAACP), a group of thirteen parents filed a class action suit against the school board of Topeka, Kansas (Cozzens, 1995).

On May 17, 1954, the Supreme Court ruled in a unanimous decision that the "separate but equal" clause was unconstitutional because it violated the Fourteenth Amendment by separating schools based solely on the classification of race. Chief Justice Warren delivered the court's opinion, stating: "Segregated schools are not equal and cannot be made equal, and hence they are deprived of the equal protection of the laws" (Cozzens,

1995). The ruling in favor of integration is one of the most significant strides America has taken in favor of civil liberties. It remains, to this day, as the most pivotal and recognized court decision of its era.

Although the unanimous ruling declared segregation in education to be inherently unequal, many southern politicians regarded the decision as a "clear abuse of judicial power," and ten years after the case, only one percent of black students in the South attended desegregated schools. The lawyer who took on this case was Thurgood Marshall, a key civil rights leader during the 1950s and 1960s. A distinguished lawyer, Marshall specialized in civil rights cases and was admitted to practice before the U.S. Supreme Court in 1939, where he won 29 of the 32 cases. Marshall also served the NAACP as special counsel for 12 years and helped lead it to numerous significant victories. He was appointed by President Lyndon B. Johnson as the first black member of the Supreme Court in October of 1967 (Family Education Network, 2003). *Brown v. Board of Education* changed America forever, but the change from segregated schools did not come without active protest. Southern activists and politicians resisted the potential revolution and provided ample opposition to prevent integration in what they considered to be their states (Cozzens, 1995).

In December 1955, Rosa Parks, an American civil rights activist and longtime member of the NAACP in Alabama, was arrested for refusing to relinquish her seat in the so-called "white" section of a city bus. This violation of the Fourteenth Amendment motivated Dr. Martin Luther King, Jr. to lead a boycott of public transportation. This boycott lasted successfully for over a year, and helped lift Dr. King to national prominence as a main, and possibly the most influential civil-rights leader this country has ever seen (Family Education Network, 1995).

In 1956 the University of Alabama admitted its first black student, Autherine Lucy, as ordered by the Birmingham Federal Court. Following her admittance, she was attacked and assaulted on the school campus by an angry mob of KKK members and segregationists. Lucy was later suspended and expelled from the school for allegedly partaking in an NAACP conspiracy. That same year, a federal court ruling ended intrastate segregation on public transportation. Dr. King boarded the first integrated bus in Montgomery (Family Education Network, 1995).

In September of 1957 President Eisenhower was forced to send the National Guard to Little Rock, Arkansas, to protect four black students threatened by segregationists. To make matters worse the governor of Arkansas was prohibiting integration. Also in 1957, Dr. King became the leader of the Southern Christian Leadership Council, adding to his exceptionally active role in the fight for civil rights (Family Education Network, 1995).

A relative calm settled in during the last two years of the 1950s, and it was not until the introduction of peaceful sit-ins that the waters began to ripple once again. On February 1, 1960, a group of North Carolina students from the Students Nonviolent Coordination Committee (SNCC) conducted the first sit-in. Following this act, sit-ins rapidly spread throughout the south. A more notable sit-in took place at North Carolina's A&T University, when four boys in search of a meal took their seats at a segregated lunch counter. They were refused service by the white employees but continued to peacefully wait until the store closed. After being blatantly disregarded, the boys returned the next day with 25 other students, only to have their requests denied once again. These four boys became icons for the civil rights movement when the cold responses to these peaceful protests fueled the drive for impartiality (Family Education Network, 1995).

The vitality of segregation was put to a test in 1961, when the Congress of Racial Equality (CORE) began sending student volunteers on bus trips to assess the implications of the newly implemented segregation laws pertaining to interstate travel. The "Freedom Riders," as they were called, organized and rode through the southern states to scrutinize segregation in various bus terminals. There were six hundred marshals deployed to protect these riders (Family Education Network, 1995).

Also in 1961, James Meredith applied for enrollment at the University of Mississippi only to have his admission declined by telegram. He sent a letter to the Department of Justice requesting assistance. Meredith continued to write the university requesting that his application be considered for the summer session until finally, on May 31, 1961, the NAACP Legal Defense and Educational Fund filed suit in the U.S. District Court. The suit alleged that Meredith was refused admission to the university based solely on his race. After numerous legal battles and appeals, the United States Supreme Court forced the University of Mississippi to admit James Meredith. President John F. Kennedy was forced to send guardsmen to combat the ensuing riots at the university (Family Education Network, 1995).

Another right blacks were denied was the right to an equal education in public schools. Governor Wallace of Alabama, in his inauguration speech, went as far as saying that it would be "segregation now, segregation tomorrow, segregation forever," and he vowed to stand in the schoolhouse door (Cooper and Terrill, 2002). President Kennedy announced a settlement that provided for desegregation of public facilities and lunch counters and for improvements in job opportunities (Cooper and Terrill, 2002). Despite the progress made by Kennedy, there were still states that were not integrating their public schools. Governor Wallace epitomized separatism as he attempted to keep the schools segregated; however, the federal government eventually defeated his attempts. In fact, the government had two black students escorted to class by federal officials. On September 15, white supremacists planted a bomb in a Birmingham Baptist Church, which killed four girls and seriously injured a fifth. Three months prior to this incident, Governor Wallace prevented black students from enrolling at the University of Alabama. Wallace eventually surrendered to the Assistant Attorney General and the Alabama National Guard (Cooper and Terrill, 2002).

To further address the issue of segregation in education, Congress wrote Title IV in 1965. Title IV focused on desegregation of public education. This act gave the Commissioner of Education two years to survey the opportunities of equal education for individuals of different race, religion, or national origin and to report the results to the President and Congress. There were grants the Commissioner could give to teachers and school personnel for training on desegregation, and if needed, Desegregation Problem Specialists could be hired (Loevy, 1997).

On August 28, 1963, Dr. King presented his "I Have a Dream" speech. The speech was preceded by a march to the Lincoln Memorial in Washington. Over 250,000 people joined him that day (Ayres, 1993). This march would be known later as one of the largest civil rights demonstrations in history (Ayres, 1993). People who attended the march ranged from dignitaries to commoners. The speech that Dr. King delivered to the crowd that day was not the speech he had intended on giving. He had worked for two days previous to the march on the speech he was going to give, but, when it was time to give his speech, the energy he received from the crowd made him change his mind. He gave his speech on The Dream. Following the speech and march, King and other African American leaders met with President Kennedy (Ayres, 1993).

Not only were blacks denied their right to equal education, many were unable to exercise their right to vote. There was not a high number of them actually registered. Despite Title I of the 1964 Civil Rights Act and statutes passed to help give blacks the equal right to vote, Title I allowed law officers to use any standard, procedure, or practice that was different from the state laws or Federal voting laws to determine who was eligible to vote. Individuals could be denied voting rights based on mistakes on any type of record related to applications or registration for voting (Loevy, 1997).

During the Freedom Summer of 1964, which was an event in Mississippi to help blacks register to vote, three college students were murdered for their participation in the event. The event drew over two hundred students but unfortunately ended in anguish. Blacks who fought for their right to vote were brutalized in 1965 during a demonstration at a Methodist Church in Alabama. This demonstration was intended to be peaceful. White policemen and civilians clubbed and beat the demonstrators. One young man was even shot and killed (Ayers, 1993). The boy's memorial service was organized by Dr. King and the Southern Christian Leadership Council. They led a march from Selma to the Capitol in Montgomery. Due to orders from Governor Wallace, there were state troopers and civilian vigilantes posted at the Pettus Bridge, waiting to ambush the marchers with toxic tear gas, whips and billy clubs. As a nationwide audience watched, the brutal attacks resulted in the hospitalization of 50 marchers. For this struggle, the media adopted the name "Bloody Sunday." In March 1965, Dr. King and 3,000 others marched to the State Capitol. There they were joined by tens of thousands of supporters. The march ended with Dr. King addressing the crowd's concern for how long freedom would take. He reassured them that, in the end, there would be justice. Finally, in 1965, blacks were allowed the right to vote.

During 1967, blacks were able to register to vote (Ayers, 1993). In 1964, the Civil Rights act gave:

> The constitutional right to vote, to confer jurisdiction upon the district courts of the United States to provide injunctive relief against discrimination in public accommodations, to authorize the Attorney general to institute suits to protect constitutional rights in public facilities and public education, to extend the commission on Civil Rights, to prevent discrimination in federally assisted programs, to establish a commission on Equal Employment Opportunity, and for other purposes (Loevy, 1997).

Under this Civil Rights Act of 1964, Title VI stated that programs and activities that received federal financial assistance from the department of education could not deny participation or benefits to people based on their race, color, or national origin. If programs and activities violated the act, they would risk losing all federal assistance (Loevy, 1997).

Dr. King once said, "There was always a strict enforcement of the 'separate' without the slightest intention to abide by the 'equal.'" Still, he would go on to articulate that, even if "equal" were established, it would merely be a delusion. Innate in separatism is inequality because separation deprives people of experiences which only integration can provide. Since the assassination of Dr. King on April 4, 1968, the realm of civil rights has continued to rise and fall in an often rewarding but also torturously inconsistent manner. From the ups in the late 1960s and 1980s, to the downs in the 1970s and 2000s, it is due time for this ride to make a permanent ascent to the pinnacle of human rights.

The closure of the 1960s and the beginning of the 1970s saw several influential court cases that promoted integration. *Green v. County School Board of New Kent County*, 1968, in Virginia, stated that schools deemed segregated were to be dismantled on every level. This would come to be called a "unitary" status. Yet the "freedom of choice" that districts were given to desegregate did not result in a substantial amount of desegregation, which was the primary drive for this case. A similar ruling was established in Mississippi with the *Alexander v. Holmes* case a year later (New Jersey Professional Education Port (NJPEP), 2004). Charlotte, North Carolina saw a pivotal case go to the Supreme Court in 1971. *Swann v. Charlotte-Mecklenburg Board of Education* determined that busing could and would be used to transport students in from outside areas in order to promote more integration, in a thorough and prompt manner (Orfield & Lee, 2004).

With the findings of these court cases, the fight for desegregation seemed to be heading in the right direction. It was as if the mindsets of people were beginning to change and equality was beginning to emerge on a very broad scale. It felt that way at least, until 1974. In *Milliken v. Bradley* in 1974 in Detroit, Michigan, was the regression to an old decline in the fight for equality. The Supreme Court found that, if suburban areas did not illegally contribute to the segregation in its neighboring city, those suburban districts could not be forced to assist in the desegregation efforts of that city, as they were of the mindset that desegregation was a form of unfair punishment to suburbs (NJPEP, 2004). Justice Marshall, of the Supreme Court, voiced his dissent of this decision by saying, "After 20 years of small, often difficult steps toward that great end, the court today takes a giant step backwards... The very evil that Brown was aimed at will not be cured, but will be perpetuated for the future (NJPEP, 2004)."

The court's failure to acknowledge or to learn from the past would continue in *Milliken v. Bradley II*, 1977. This case completed the "separate but equal" notion by granting lower courts the power to demand additional funding in order to offset any possible discrepancies established by segregation (NJPEP, 2004). It was as if "separate but equal" had never been tried and had never failed some eighty years before. This inexplicable ruling led to the erosion of so many hard fought battles in the 1960s. It was caused by the narrow vision of those in power.

In the midst of these regressions in the northern United States, the south had slowly continued to improve on its segregation during the 1980s. Part of this is believed to be due to the decline in residential segregation.

Communities not only began to integrate schools, but also to live together, slowly ascending toward the goal of equality and integration. Slowly, progress was again being made (Orfield & Lee, 2004).

In the early 1990s, as things appeared to be, again, headed in the right direction, inexplicably the Supreme Court made numerous attempts to re-segregate neighborhood schools in the south. *Board of Education of Oklahoma v. Dowell* in 1991 allowed communities to revert back to segregation so long as these communities had achieved the unitary status established in *Green v. New Kent County*. According to the court, desegregation orders were temporary and a return to segregated unitary neighborhood schools was acceptable, eliminating the need for further court supervision (NJPEP, 2004). A year later in *Freeman v. Pitts* the Supreme Court established that:

> If a school system subject to a court-supervised desegregation plan is in compliance in some but not all areas, the court, in appropriate cases, may return control to the school system in those areas where compliance has been achieved, limiting further judicial supervision to operations that are not yet in full compliance with the court decree (NJPEP, 2004).

In other words, if a school district had complied with court demands of desegregation in some areas, it would be up to the Court to decide if it would free the district of the Court's guidance in the effort toward desegregation. If this were established, the local courts would then take over in the supervision of such districts.

Essentially, what came to fruition in the 1990s was the removal of the Court's assistance in desegregation efforts. They were easing their way out with what seemed to be one of two agendas; they either felt that society had firmly established desegregation and could uphold such a notion on its own, or the idea of "separate but equal" deserved another opportunity to fail. Either way, this ignorant decision would prove to be a trigger for the recession of civil rights.

A deeper look into statistics regarding segregation supports this idea of inconsistency in efforts to achieve civil rights over the past 25 years, a time in which many people have assumed that, in the struggle for an all-encompassing equality, our work is done. This is not the case. The number of black students in predominantly white southern schools mirrors this pattern of inconsistency. In the wake of the civil rights movements in the late 1960s, the number of black students in white schools increased by almost 15 times in six years and eventually reached its high mark in 1988. The pain and suffering of the pioneers of civil rights was finally paying off with resounding results when 44 percent of black students filled majority white schools in the south. It was a time, 15 years ago, when integration for blacks in the south, at least by the numbers, had been achieved (Orfield & Lee, 2004). However, since 1988, the percentage of black students in majority white schools in the south has consistently dropped; in 2001 it was at 30 percent, a number unparalleled since 1969. In fact, the percentage of black and Latino students in minority schools in all regions of the continental United States, without exception, increased in the 1990s (Orfield & Lee, 2004). Let it not be deemed coincidental that the lack of effort applied toward desegregation and the rise in separation walked hand-in-hand in the 1990s. From this point on, should the problem endure, let it not be deemed incidental. When racial discrimination is accepted by the majority, reversing its effects has proven to be an arduous process.

FEDERAL COURT SYSTEM

The federal court system consists of the United States Supreme Court, the United States Courts of Appeals, the U.S. District Courts, and special purpose courts. Only the Supreme Court was established by the United States Constitution. The other courts were established by acts of Congress. The United States District Courts are trial courts. The Circuit Courts of Appeals are appellate courts. The Supreme Court is essentially an appellate court, even though it is given "original jurisdiction" to hear controversies between states and cases involving foreign issues.

The federal courts hear civil and criminal cases involving federal laws. They also hear cases that involve individuals or groups from different states. Federal courts are referred to as U.S. District Courts. If one is to lose a case in the U.S. District Court, that person has the opportunity to appeal to the U.S Circuit Court of Appeals in his or her region. In the U.S. we have 13 circuit courts. See diagram on page 14.

The state court systems are designed and structured like the federal courts. Every state in the union has trial courts. The courts are known as Superior and Municipal Courts. The trial courts deal with issues involving family, traffic, small claims, criminal acts and probates. Cases dealing with juveniles and family disputes are heard in the Family Court. Under certain circumstances, cases involving juveniles are heard in Juvenile Court. Actions involving violation of traffic are heard in the Traffic Court. Cases involving wills and claims against the estate of an individual who passed away without leaving a will is handled by the Probate Court. The Criminal Court handles cases involving crimes that will cause the violator to be sentenced to jail.

Depending on the outcome of a case, the parties may appeal to the Circuit Court or the State Supreme Court. If the case appealed to the State Supreme Court deals with state law, it cannot be appealed any further.

The 13 Federal Judicial Circuits

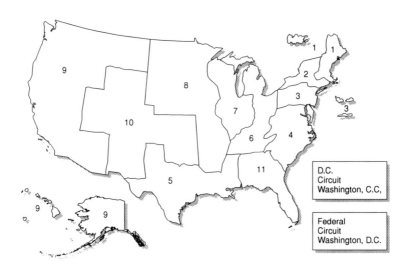

The D.C. and Federal Circuits are not numbered and state lines of the map are not included.

The diagram below represents the organizational structure of the court system.

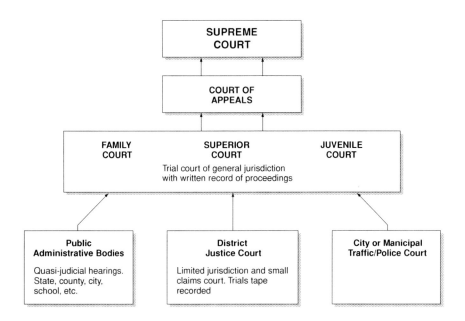

Chapter

THE UNITED STATES CONSTITUTION

In the last quarter of the 18th century there was no country in the world that governed with separated and divided powers that provided checks and balances on the exercise of authority by those who governed. The first step taken toward this was the Declaration of Independence in 1776, which was followed by the Constitution drafted in Philadelphia in 1787, and the Bill of Rights in 1791. This work of 55 men in Philadelphia marked the beginning of the end of the concept of the Divine Right of Kings.

The Federal Government is structured in accordance with the United States Constitution. The Constitution has seven articles and twenty-seven amendments. The following are excerpts from sections that concern this discussion:

AMENDMENTS

First Amendment (1791)

"Congress shall make no law respecting an establishment of religion, or prohibiting the free exercise thereof; or abridging the freedom of speech, or of the press; or the right of the people to assemble peaceably, or to petition the government for a redress of grievances…"

In theory, the rights of individuals to express themselves are absolute. In practice, however, limitations have emerged through court cases. One such limitation is libel. An individual who commits libel is not protected. If one person spreads rumors about another person that reduce the esteem of that person in a community, the person spreading the rumor may be civilly liable for slander or defamation of character. So, teachers need to pay attention to what they say about a difficult student in the teachers' lounge or to that student's potential employer.

Another limitation has to do with disruption of the peace. If a person enters a theater when a movie is in progress and shouts "fire" the mayhem that ensues could cause property damage and fatalities. Such behavior is not permissible by law. The individual will be civilly liable if not criminally liable as well.

A third limitation relates to the use of words that provoke another person to commit assault. The courts empathize and are reluctant to convict the one committing an assault because the courts frown upon deliberate provocation.

Fourth Amendment (1791)

The right of the people to be secure in their persons, houses, papers, and effects against unreasonable searches and seizures shall not be violated, and no warrants shall issue, but upon *probable cause*, supported by oath or affirmation, and the persons or things to be seized.

Fifth Amendment (1791)

No person shall be held to answer for a capital or otherwise infamous crime unless on a presentment or indictment of a grand jury, except in cases arising in the land or naval forces, or in the militia when in actual service in time of war or public danger; nor shall any person be subject for the same offense and be twice put in jeopardy of life or limb; nor shall a person be compelled in any criminal case to be a witness against himself, nor be deprived of life, liberty, or property, without due process of law; nor shall private property be taken for public use without just compensation. *can't be charged or deprived of rights, until proven guilty*

Tenth Amendment (1791)

The powers not delegated to the United States by the Constitution, nor prohibited by it to the states, are reserved to the states respectively, or to the people.

Fourteenth Amendment (1868)

All persons born or naturalized in the United States and subject to the jurisdiction thereof are citizens of the United States and of the states wherein they reside. No state shall make or enforce any law which shall abridge the privileges or immunities of citizens of the United States; nor shall any state deprive any person of life, liberty, or property without due process of the law; nor deny to any person within its jurisdiction the equal protection of the law.

Fifteenth Amendment (1870)

The right of citizens of the United States to vote shall not be denied or abridged by the United States or by any State on account of race, color, or previous condition of servitude.

THE LEGAL PROCEDURES

A brief explanation of legal procedures sheds light on the judicial role in the state system of education. Most laws are very clear. They direct state and public officials to carry out certain duties that are clearly defined. For example, the laws are clear about providing schools for all children. Most state court systems consist of three levels: trial courts (where cases begin), appellate courts (where most appeals from the trial courts are held), and the state supreme court of last resort (where the final decisions are made about cases).

Civil cases begin when a plaintiff files a complaint against a defendant. Evidence pertaining to the dispute is introduced. The judge in a non-jury proceeding, or a jury, reaches a verdict, and the court renders an opinion. If either party is not satisfied with the decision, either one or both parties may appeal to an appellate court.

An appellate court's mandate is to review decisions made by lower district courts and to decide whether the judgments can stand on legal merit or should be overturned on some point of law. An appellate court has no power to hear the case until the trial court has reached a final decision. An appellate court does not hear testimony. It reviews the recorded trial proceedings and may either affirm or reverse the trial court's decision or, in some cases, send the case back to the trial court for further hearing. An appellate court's decision is usually final. Although the State Supreme (or final) Court has the power to hear almost any case, this court actually hears a very small percentage of the cases begun at the trial court level. Most cases are not of such public importance as to justify the time and expense of appeal to the highest state court.

The State Supreme Court generally takes appeals from appellate court decisions. In some states, however, certain types of cases may be appealed directly from the trial court to the highest state court. The Supreme Court sets the rules by which it hears appeals from lower courts. Some cases may be started in the State Supreme Court, bypassing the trial court altogether. The Illinois constitution, for example, provides that the State Supreme Court shall have original jurisdiction in "cases relating to revenue, mandamus, prohibition and habeas corpus... and only appellate jurisdiction in other cases."

Most cases involving schools are civil, rather than criminal matters. Civil cases involve alleged wrongs against the individual; criminal cases arise from alleged wrongs against the state. Cases concerning school matters frequently go through the federal court system to the United States Supreme Court. The Supreme Court picks and chooses the cases it hears. Unless the Court believes the case involves an important federal or national issue, it will not hear the matter. The issues in such cases touch upon rights guaranteed by the federal constitution or affected by federal legislation. During the past two decades, cases concerning segregation, saluting the flag, church-state relations, and other civil-rights issues have been decided by the Supreme Court.

Once a case is before the Supreme Court, its task is to interpret the law using the facts at hand. In school matters, the Court carefully refrains from legislating school policies and recasting school legislation. If the matter has come before a court in an earlier case, the doctrine of *stare decisis* (abide by or follow decided cases) guides its decision-making process. This doctrine, also known as *the rule of precedent*, removes some of the guesswork from lawsuits and serves as a guide to both litigants and the Court.

Many cases involve a school board's discretion in making policies and procedures for schools. As the cases demonstrate, the court looks to the reasonableness of the school board's actions and rarely substitutes its wisdom for that of the board members. Because of the peculiar and awesome responsibility placed on the school boards, courts are most reluctant to overturn the boards' decisions unless they clearly breach either the manifest intent of the law or the bounds of reason.

THE CONSTITUTION AND SCHOOLS

The First Amendment to the United States Constitution states that "Congress shall make no law respecting an establishment of religion, or prohibiting the free exercise thereof." Like the Fourth Amendment, the First has been applied to the states via the Fourteenth Amendment.

Since the creation of the Constitution, a majority of court decisions and laws that have influenced public education originate from amendments to the Constitution. Another provision in the Constitution, which is significant to teachers, is Article 1, Section 10. This is a contract clause that reads: "No state shall enter into any treaty, alliance, or confederation; grant letters of marque and reprisal; coin money; emits bills of credit; make any thing but gold and silver coin a tender in payment of debts; pass any bill of attainder, ex post facto law, or law impairing the obligation of contracts, or grant any title of nobility...." This speaks to the guaranteed rights concerning tenure, retirement, and other benefits.

In the United States Constitution, the First Amendment is frequently cited as insuring individual rights. One guarantee the First Amendment ensures is that "Congress shall make no law respecting an establishment of religion or prohibiting the free exercise thereof." The Constitution of the United States did not specifically mention education. The Tenth Amendment, at the same time, states that "the powers not delegated to the United States by the Constitution, nor prohibited by it to the States, are reserved to the States respectively, or to the people." Since the federal constitution never mentioned schools, the power and responsibility for public education became the responsibility of the States or the people.

The administration of public education is the responsibility of each state. Due to restrictions imposed by the state and federal constitution, state legislatures create, fund, and regulate public schools, intermediates, and local agencies. The state legislatures make available school financial support, curriculum, certification for teachers and administrators, and policies. The operational decisions are made by the local board members that are elected by voters in the school district.

According to Hazard (1978), "Control of public education" means little in the abstract; there are levels of control and many contextual meanings.

The following diagram explains the sources of legal control over the schools.

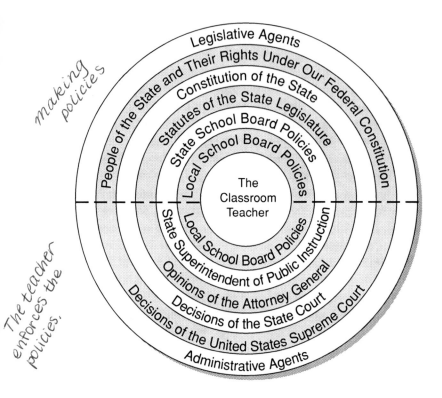

The diagram is adapted from Dr. Floyd Edwards' lecture notes, East Tennessee State University.

PRAYER IN SCHOOL

"Congress shall make no law respecting an establishment of religion or prohibiting the free exercise thereof." According to the American Civil Liberties Union, these opening words to the First Amendment to the Constitution set forth a dual guarantee of religious liberty. Both the Establishment Clause and the Free Exercise Clause operate to protect religious liberty and freedom of conscience for all Americans. Quoting Thomas Jefferson, the Supreme Court has stated that the Establishment Clause was intended to accomplish this end by erecting a "wall of separation between church and state." (*Everson v. Board of Educ. of Ewing*, 330 U.S. 1, 15-16, 1947).

It is one of the fundamental principles of the Supreme Court's Establishment of Clause Jurisprudence that the Constitution forbids not only state practices that "aid one religion over another," but also those practices that "aid all religions" and thus endorse or prefer religion to nonreligion. In light of the U.S. Supreme Court's stand on the Establishment Clause, a landmark ruling was made in 1962 in the case of *Engle v. Vitale*. The Supreme Court ruled in *Engle v. Vitale* 370 U.S. (1952), that the use of the nonsectarian prayer composed by the New York State Board of Regents and recommended for daily recitation in the New York Schools violated the Establishment Clause. The prayer in question read: "**Almighty God, we acknowledge our dependence upon Thee, and we beg Thy blessings upon us, our parents, our teachers and our country.**" The Court held by a six-to-one vote that the use of the prayer violated the "Establishment Clause even though the prayer was non-denominational and its observance on the part of the students was voluntary."

Justice Black delivered the opinion of the Court by saying: "There is no doubt that New York's program of daily classroom invocation of God's blessings as prescribed in the Regents' prayer is a religious activity. It is a solemn avowal of divine faith and supplication for the blessings of the almighty... [S]tate laws requiring or permitting use of the Regents' prayer must be struck down as a violation of the Establishment Clause because that prayer was composed by governmental officials as part of a governmental program to further religious beliefs."

In the case of *Abington v. Schempp*, 374 U.S. 203 (1963), as their classmates stood and recited the Lord's Prayer to begin the school day, Roger and Donna Schempp fumed. They tried to close their ears when the intercom system boomed Bible verses into their homeroom at Abington Senior High.

Roger and Donna and their parents, because of their personal religious beliefs, objected to these exercises that took place daily in the Abington, Pennsylvania, public schools. The family filed a lawsuit in a federal district court to stop the School District of Abington from conducting the prayers and readings, which were required by state law. The Pennsylvania statute stated: "At least ten verses from the Holy Bible shall be read, without comment, at the opening of each public school on each school day. Any child shall be excused from such Bible reading upon the written request of his parent or guardian. The Schempps argued that this law violated their constitutional rights under the First Amendment.

At the trial, the Schempps claimed that the classroom exercises involved a literal reading of the Bible. And this, they said, conveyed doctrines contrary to their religious beliefs. One witness, an expert on Judaism, testified that parts of the New Testament would be offensive to Jews, and if read in class without explanation could be harmful to Jewish students. Another expert witness, a Protestant scripture scholar, said that the Bible was nonsectarian, but only among Christian faiths.

Mr. Schempp testified that he had decided not to have his children excused from the Bible reading even though the law allowed it. He contended that this would have hurt their relationships with their teachers and classmates. If Roger and Donna had been excused, they would have to stand in the hallway outside the classroom. They would have felt like "oddballs" or looked as though they were being punished.

The school district argued that the Bible, because of its great literary, historical, and moral value, was an important part of any educational program. It offered non-religious values useful to society. Besides, unless the schools provided some religious exercises, they would seem to foster a "religion of secularism" and actually be hostile toward religion. The school district added that Americans have historically been a religious people. It cited recent figures indicating that 64 percent of U.S. citizens belonged to a church, while only three percent professed no religion at all.

A federal district court held that the Pennsylvania statute requiring Bible reading in the public schools violated the First Amendment, as applied to the states by the Fourteenth Amendment. The court said this was true in spite of the provision for excusing a student from the reading. The Abington School District appealed to the U.S. Supreme Court. The Supreme Court ruled "While the Free Exercise Clause clearly prohibits the use of state action to deny the rights of free exercise to anyone, it has never meant that a majority could use the machinery of the state to practice its beliefs (Justice Clark, *School District of Abington v. Schempp*, 1963 p. 24).

To the basic inquiry of whether or not governmental activity preserves neutrality regarding matters of religious belief, modern Establishment Clause cases do establish the premise that the Clause forbids promotion of religion generally, not just promotion of one sect over another.

In other instances, funding programs have presented difficult issues regarding neutral programs that benefit religious activities. The New Jersey statute authorizing school districts to transport all students of public and parochial schools was held to be constitutional in *Everson v. Board of Education*, 330 U.S. 1 (1947). Also, the Louisiana statute which made provisions for free textbooks out of public funds to private school students was found to be constitutional in *Cochran v. Louisiana State Board of Education* 50 Sup. Ct. 335 (1930).

The arguments in *Everson v. Board of Education* and *Cochran v. Louisiana State Board of Education*, were that extension of services such as busing, tuition assistance, textbooks, and services to parochial schools are generally permissible under the *Child Benefit Doctrine*. That is, schools may provide assistance to children in private schools but no benefits to the parochial or religious schools. However, the courts at times have invalidated programs, requiring government supervision to insure non-sectarian use of funds. Before 1970, in measuring whether a state action had violated the Establishment Clause, the Supreme Court sought to determine state neutrality with a two-part test requiring that the secular purpose of the action of the state not be to aid one religion or all religions and the primary effect of the program be one that neither advances nor inhibits religion. In 1970 the Supreme Court added a third prong to the test that states must not foster excessive governmental entanglement with religion.

In 1971 the Supreme Court fused these three criteria and applied them to strike down salary supplements to teachers in private schools and the purchase of educational services in private schools *Lemon v. Kurtzman*, 403 U.S. 602 (1971). The three-part test criteria are now known as the **Lemon Test**. The *Lemon v. Kurtzman* case raised questions about whether or not state aid should go to church related schools for secular purposes. In 1968, Pennsylvania enacted a statute that authorized the state to reimburse non-public schools specifically for their actual expenditures on teacher salaries, textbooks, and instructional materials that are used for secular courses. Also, in 1969, Rhode Island enacted a salary supplement act that provided for a 15 percent salary supplement for teachers in non-public schools in which the average cost per student in secular education was below the average in the public schools. The teachers receiving this supplement would be certified to teach only courses offered in the public schools and to use only instructional materials used in the public schools. Also, in writing, teachers had to agree not to teach any course in religion.

In 1971, Lemon, a tax paying citizen and parent of a child attending a public school in Pennsylvania argued that he should not have to pay a specific tax that supports non-public schools. Seven church-affiliated schools defended this statute and the taxing of non-public schools. Questions raised in *Lemon v. Kurtzman* are whether it is unconstitutional for the state to provide subsidies for non-public school teachers' salaries even when the funds are paid only to teachers of secular subjects and whether it is unconstitutional for a state to reimburse non-public schools for expenses incurred in the teaching of secular subjects.

The decision was that both statutes were unconstitutional under the Establishment Clause of the First Amendment because they created an excessive entanglement between government and religion. In order for a statute to be valid, it must have a secular legislative purpose and a principle effect which neither advances nor inhibits religion, and it must not foster an excessive government entanglement with religion. As in the case of Rhode Island, state subsidized teachers would have to be monitored extensively by the state to assure that they did not teach religion, and this would involve an excessive entanglement between church and state. As in the case of Pennsylvania, aid would be given directly to the non-public schools. This, combined with the surveillance and accounting procedures that would be required, would create excessive church-state entanglement and excessive state support of religion. The court has applied these three criteria since Lemon.

A great deal of establishment litigation involves public schools. This is a matter of particular concern because public tax money supports these schools and their activities. Of even greater concern is the impressionable nature of children and the compulsory school attendance machinery that coerces children to be in school and participate in school activities. Coercing children to participate in religious activities is highly offensive to our free society.

In summary, establishment cases have been centered on attempts to inject religion into the schools by prayer sessions, "moments of silence," religious holiday observances in classrooms, religious speakers at school assemblies and graduations, and curriculum alterations that support religious beliefs.

THE FREE EXERCISE CLAUSE (1st Amend.)

According to John Carroll, the Free Exercise Clause is particularly interesting because it has been a constitutional flash point under which highly charged issues have been adjudicated: "Under free exercise the nation has attempted to define what the idea of religious toleration means, that is, the degree to which members of dominant religious groups must allow the unconventional practices of religious minorities." Carroll further states that it is always religious minorities, and often detested minorities, who seek refuge under its protections. Federal law concerning religion and schools stems from the Free Exercise Clause of the First Amendment. In regard to this Free Exercise Clause, "congress shall not prohibit the free exercise of religion." Although the Supreme Court has ruled that an individual or group has an absolute right to hold and advocate any religious belief, the right to act on those beliefs is not absolute.

To examine the Free Exercise Clause it is necessary to pay some attention to strategies of constitutional interpretation because such strategies structure the way judges and scholars have thought about the clause. One of the many strategies is to analyze original intent. Those who believe that the Clause should be interpreted in light of the framers' intent sometimes reach different conclusions from those who believe that the framers' intent is unfathomable or even irrelevant. However, religion has been seen as a rival of the state in its allegiance to God. Consequently, a state that actively competes with religion for the allegiance of its citizens is likely to be at a risk. While it may win in the short run through legislation, it may suffer the disaffection of those it has opposed. According to Carroll, when government enters the religious arena, it places itself on ground where everything is contested. There is no agreement on whether God exists among persons of faith, let alone between believers and non-believers. The various religious groups also disagree about the characteristics of God, who God is or was, what God requires of people for them to be saved, and whether salvation is possible for all or some. Nor is there agreement about whether life exists after death and the form, if any, that life takes, the relationship between God and human beings, the definition of ritual, how God can be known, how God can or must be worshipped or served, and so on. While some persons take the position that what you believe is less important than belief itself, others disagree. In fact, most firmly believe there is a religious truth of which they or their group is the keeper.

Due to these different beliefs, the Free Exercise Clause has had effects on school policies and student behavior. School curriculum requirements frequently conflict with parents' religious beliefs. Many parents, for example, object to their children studying theories of evolution on the premise that such courses interfere with the free exercise of their religion. Public expression of patriotism through classroom activities, such as saluting the flag, has also prompted parents to object on the basis of the Free Exercise Clause.

A classic example is the case of *West Virginia State Board of Education v. Barnette*, 319 U.S. 624, 63 S. Ct. 1178 (1949), regarding the compulsory flag salute. The issues under consideration were whether the government could require students to do anything that is offensive to their religious belief, whether a compulsory flag salute statute is unconstitutional, and whether requiring students to salute the flag when it is forbidden by their religion violates the Free Exercise Clause of the First Amendment.

Two Jehovah's Witness students refused to salute the flag because doing so was against their religious belief that forbids them to bow down to or to serve graven images. The West Virginia Board of Education, during World War II, ordered that the flag salute become a regular part of school program activities. The students' parents offered substitute pledges that did not make the flag an image, but the state refused. As a result the students were expelled, and the parents were faced with prosecution for causing their children's delinquency. The students sued the West Virginia State Board of Education in violation of their First Amendment rights. The Federal District Court ruled in favor of the students. Then, the West Virginia School Board appealed the case to an appellate court, where the decision of the lower court was affirmed. The West Virginia School Board further appealed to the United States Supreme Court and, again, the decision was affirmed.

The reasoning for the affirmations was that students may not be compelled to pledge allegiance to the flag in public schools. The First Amendment protects the students' rights not to salute the flag or recite the Pledge of Allegiance. The Supreme Court's decision was six to three. When Justice Jackson delivered the opinion of the court, he stated that: "compulsory flag salute is a futile attempt at coherence." He emphasized that the "Bill of Rights denies to those in power any legal opportunity to coerce the consent of the governed: If there is any fixed star in our constitutional constellation, it is that no official, high or petty, can prescribe what shall be orthodox in politics, nationalism, religion, or other matters of opinion, or force citizens to confess by word or act their faith therein." Therefore, compulsory flag salutes are considered unconstitutional now, and the result of this case stands as a great civil liberties precedent.

In Washington State, school districts are required to hold appropriate flag exercises in each classroom at the beginning of the school day for students who desire to recite the salute of allegiance RCW 28A.230.140. State law, however, provides no penalties for teachers who refuse to lead the flag salute. Teachers have a constitutional right to refuse to participate in flag exercises (*Russo v. Central School District No. 1*, 469 F.2d 623 (2d Cir. 1972), cert. Denied, 411 U.S. 932 (1973).

School-prayer cases have raised dilemmas for many people. The establishment and Free Exercise Clauses of the First Amendment are not disjunctive but complementary. To ban the establishment of religion (as seen by one) is to interfere with another's free exercise of religion. The prayer ban sustains the parent who fears governmental establishment of religion, but it frustrates the free exercise of religion by pro-prayer parents. Non-sectarian practices in schools are generally suspect. Religious holiday observances are viewed also with suspicion by the United States Supreme Court.

FREE SPEECH IN SCHOOL

The Supreme Court has traditionally viewed First Amendment rights in the schools as a balancing of individual interests in free expression against the day-to-day administration of schools. "The U.S. Supreme Court has repeatedly emphasized the need for affirming the comprehensive authority of the states and of school officials, consistent with fundamental constitutional safeguards, to prescribe and control conduct in the schools.... Our problem lies in the area where students, in the exercise of First Amendment rights, collide with the rules of the school authorities (p. 6)."

An example is in the case of *Tinker v. Des Moines Community Independent School District No. 21*, 89 S. Ct. 733 (1969). Petitioners John F. Tinker, 15 years old, and Christopher Eckhardt, 16 years old, attended high schools in Des Moines. Petitioner Mary Beth Tinker, John's sister, 13 years old, attended junior high school. In December, 1965, a group of adults and students in Des Moines, Iowa, held a meeting at the Eckhardt home. The group determined to publicize their objection to the hostilities in Vietnam and their support for a truce by wearing black armbands during the holiday season and by fasting on December 16 and New Year's Eve. The petitioners and their parents had previously engaged in similar activities, and they decided to participate in this activity. The Principals of the Des Moines schools became aware of this plan and on December 14, 1965, they met and adopted a policy that students wearing armbands would be asked to remove them, and if they refused, they would be suspended until they returned without the armbands. The petitioners were aware of the regulation adopted by the school authorities. On December 16, Mary Beth and Christopher Tinker wore black armbands to their schools. John Tinker wore his armband the next day. They were all sent home and suspended from school until they decided to come back without their armbands. They did not return to school until after their planned period for wearing armbands had expired.

A complaint was filed in the United States District Court by the petitioners, through their fathers, under 1983 of Title 42 of the United States Code. They asked for an injunction restraining the defendant school officials and the defendant members of the Board of Directors of the school district from disciplining the petitioners, and they sought nominal damages. After an evidentiary hearing the District Court dismissed the complaint. It upheld the constitutionality of the school authorities' action on the ground that it was reasonable in order to prevent disturbance of school discipline (258 F. Supp. 971 (1966)). The court referred to but expressly declined to follow the Fifth Circuit's holding in a similar case that prohibition of wearing of symbols like armbands cannot be sustained unless it "materially and substantially interfere[s] with the requirements of appropriate discipline in the operation of the school" (*Burnside v. Byars*, 363 F. 2d 744,749 (1966)).

On appeal, the Court of Appeals for the Eighth Circuit considered the case enbanc. The court was equally divided, so the District Court's decision was affirmed, without opinion (383 F. 2d 988 (1967)), and granted certiorari (390 U.S. 942 (1968)). The District Court recognized that wearing of armbands for the purpose of expressing views is a symbolic act that is within the Free Speech Clause of the First Amendment.

First Amendment rights, applied in light of special characteristics of the school environment, are available to teachers and students. It can hardly be argued that either students or teachers shed their constitutional rights to freedom of speech or expression at the schoolhouse gate. This has been the unmistakable holding of the Supreme Court for almost 50 years. In *Meyer v. Nebraska*, 262 U.S. 390 (1923), and *Barrels v. Iowa*, 262 U.S. 404 (1923), Justice McReynolds stated that the Due Process Clause of the Fourteenth Amendment prevents States from forbidding the teaching of foreign language to young students. Statutes to this effect, the Court held, unconstitutionally interfere with the liberty of teachers, student, and parents. In addition, the above statement can be also deduced from the landmark *Pierce v. Society of Sisters*, 268 U.S. 510 (1925). Ruling in favor of the students in the Tinker case, the Supreme Court held that school authorities might regulate expression of students' points of view only upon showing an actual or predictable threat and substantial interference in the operation of the school.

In recent years, the United States Supreme Court has revisited the issue of student First Amendment rights, and most times, it has ruled in favor of school administrators. In *Hazelwood School District v. Kuhlmier*, 484 U.S. 260 (1988), student staff members of the school newspaper filed suit in Federal District Court against the Hazlewood School District and school officials, alleging that their First Amendment rights were violated by the deletion of two pages of their newspaper. The deleted pages included an article describing students' experiences with pregnancy and another discussing the impact of divorce on students at that school. The newspaper was written and edited by a journalism class as part of the school curriculum. Following school practice, the teacher in charge of the paper submitted the page proof to the school principal, who objected to the pregnancy story because the pregnant students, although not named, might be identified from the text. He also believed that the article's references to sexual activity and birth control were inappropriate reading for some young students. The principal objected to the divorce article because the page proofs he was furnished with identified the name (which was deleted by the teacher from the final version) of a student who complained about her father's conduct, and the principal believed that the student's parents should have been given an opportunity to respond to the remarks or to consent to the publication. Believing that there was no time to make necessary changes to the articles if the paper were to be issued before the end of the school year, the principal directed that the pages on which the articles appeared be withheld from publication, even though other less objectionable articles were included on these pages.

Were the First Amendment rights of the students violated? In handing down the decision, the District Court held that no First Amendment violation had occurred. The school principal acted reasonably in this case in requiring the deletion of the pregnancy article and the other articles that were to appear on the same pages of the newspaper.

Teachers should be aware that the First Amendment rights of students in public schools are not automatically coextensive with the rights of adults in other settings and must be applied in light of the special characteristics of the school environment. The school newspaper in Hazlewood cannot be characterized as a forum for public expression. School facilities may be deemed to be public forums only if school authorities have opened the facilities for indiscriminate use by the general public or by some segment of the public such as a student organization.

Another classic example is the case of *Bethel School District v. Fraser*, 106 S.Ct. 3159, 92 L. Ed.2nd 549 (1986). The school district sought to have its decision to suspend a student upheld, following an inappropriate speech he delivered. Is suspension of a student for the use of obscene or vulgar language in a public forum at school a violation of the First Amendment right to free speech? In this case, Matthew Fraser, a Bethel High School student, delivered a speech nominating a fellow student to an elective school office. As part of a school sponsored educational program in self-government, the speech was made during normal school hours at a voluntary assembly attended by about 600 students, many of whom were 14 years old. Matthew Fraser's nominating speech read as follows:

> I know a man who is firm—he's firm in his pants, he's firm in his shirt, his character is firm—but most of all, his belief in you, the students of Bethel is firm. Jeff Kuhlman is a man who takes his point and pounds it in. If necessary, he'll take an issue and nail it to the wall. He doesn't attack things in spurts, he drives hard, pushing until finally—he succeeds. Jeff is a man who will go to the very end—even the climax—for

each and every one of you. So vote for Jeff for ASB Vice President—
he'll never come between you and the best our high school can be.

Throughout his speech, the student deliberately referred to his candidate with the use of an elaborate and explicit sexual metaphor. The students' reactions to the speech varied from enthusiastic applause, with
hooting and yelling, to embarrassment and astonishment. A school coun-
selor observed student masturbation and two students simulating sexual
intercourse by movement of their hips.

Prior to delivering the speech, the student had sought the advice of
several teachers who advised against it, deeming it inappropriate. Fraser
was also made aware of a school "disruptive conduct" rule prohibiting
conduct that substantially interfered with the educational process, including the use of obscene, profane language or gestures. A day later, the Vice
Principal gave Fraser oral and written notice that his speech allegedly violated the school's disruptive conduct rule. This rule stated that: In addition to the criminal acts defined above, the commission of or participation
in certain non-criminal activities or acts may lead to disciplinary action.
Generally, these are acts which disrupt and interfere with the educational
process.

Consequently, Fraser was suspended for three days for violating the
school rule. Fraser immediately grieved the disciplinary action and en-
listed the aid of the Seattle Chapter of the American Civil Liberties Union,
which provided him with the services of a volunteer attorney. Fraser contended that his speech was not disruptive, under Tinker. To the extent
that some students reacted during the assembly, or at school the following
day, he believed that only the students causing the disruption could be
disciplined.

On May 23, 1983, Fraser filed a suit in district court alleging civil
rights claims under 42 USC 1983, for violating constitutional rights under the First and Fourteenth Amendments. He sought relief, arguing that
the disciplinary action was unconstitutional, and the school rule was vague.
At the hearing, the court ruled in favor of Fraser, stating that the suspension violated Fraser's right to free expression under the first amendment.
Also, the school's disruptive conduct rule was vague and overboard. On
September 1, 1983, the district court entered final judgment in the case,
awarding court costs, attorney's fees and damages to Fraser for violation
of his rights. The school district appealed the ruling to the Ninth Circuit
Court of Appeals.

On March 4, 1985, the Ninth Circuit, in a two-to-one decision, affirmed the district court's judgment. The majority opinion rejected the

school district's argument that Fraser's speech was disruptive according to the Tinker decision:

> Thus, what the evidence demonstrates is that Fraser's speech evoked a lively and noisy response from the students, including applause, and that a few of the students reacted with sexually suggestive movements. The administration had no difficulty in maintaining order during the assembly, and Fraser's speech did not delay the assembly program. Fraser was the second-to-last speaker, followed by his candidate, Jeff Kuhlman, who then made the final speech of the afternoon without incident. The assembly, which took place after the last school class of the day, was dismissed on schedule... Given the evidence before us, we fail to see how we can distinguish this case from Tinker on the issue of disruption. Just as the record in Tinker failed to yield evidence that the wearing of the black armbands resulted in material interference with school activity, the record now before us yields no evidence that Fraser's use of sexual innuendo in his speech materially interfered with activities at Bethel High School... In our view, a noisy response to the speech and sexually suggestive views rise to the level of a material interference with the educational process that justifies impinging upon Fraser's First Amendment rights to express himself freely.

The school district's reasoning that school administrators could regulate Fraser's speech because it was disruptive to the learning environment was rejected. The school district later authorized the filing of a petition for a writ of certiorari to the Supreme Court and petition was granted October 7, 1985. The Supreme Court then held oral arguments on March 3, 1986. On July 7, 1986, the Supreme Court issued a decision reversing the Ninth Circuit Court of Appeals.

In summary, the U.S. Supreme Court held that the Bethel School Board acted entirely within its permissible authority in suspending Fraser for his offensively lewd and indecent speech. The Court further held that this case was not the same as Tinker, where a black armband was determined to be a form of "pure speech" and not accompanied by disruptive conduct. The Fraser case included sexual innuendo that was incidental to the merits of the candidate who was being nominated for student office. The court held that "it is a highly appropriate function of public school education to prohibit the use of vulgar and offensive terms in public discourse... Schools must teach by example the shared values of a civilized social order."

The U.S. Supreme Court repeated its recognition of protecting minors from exposure to vulgar and offensive spoken language. The Court stated that a "high school assembly or classroom is no place for a sexually explicit monologue directed towards an unsuspecting audience of teenage students." The Court recognized that the school regulation and the negative reactions of two teachers gave Fraser sufficient notice that his speech might result in his suspension. One of two dissenting justices, Justice Stevens began his opinion with the famous movie quote: "Frankly, my dear, I don't give a damn." He concluded that Fraser was denied due process because he did not have sufficient notice that he would be disciplined for giving this speech.

Free Speech and Teachers

Marvin L. Pickering, a teacher at Township High School in Will County, Illinois, in 1967, brought suit against the district board for infringement of his First and Fourteenth Amendment rights of freedom of expression and due process (*Pickering v. Township High School District 205,* Will County 391 U.S. 563 (1968)). He had been dismissed from his teaching position following a review of an apparent critical letter he had submitted to the local newspaper.

In the letter, Pickering was critical of the local school board and the Superintendent's allocation of school funds between educational and athletic programs. This criticism came after two failed school bond issues. The board members reviewed his letter during a hearing process and determined that Pickering's statements were false and that the statements were detrimental to the efficient operation and administration of the school district. They dismissed Mr. Pickering pursuant to the Illinois statute.

Mr. Pickering brought suit in the circuit court of Will County. The court upheld the school board's decision to dismiss Pickering. The appellant next appealed to the Illinois Supreme Court, which again concurred with the lower court decision. Finally, Pickering appealed the decision in the U.S. Supreme Court, where the Justices reversed the lower court decision on the grounds that most of Pickering's claims in his letter were substantially correct and, further, the publishing of his letter did not create undo community pressure against the school. In sum, "we hold that in this case, absent proof of false statements knowingly or recklessly made by him, a teacher's exercise of his right to speak on issues of public importance may not furnish the basis for his dismissal from public employment. Since no such showing has been made in this case regarding the appellant's letter, his dismissal for writing it cannot be upheld, and the judgment of the Illinois Supreme Court must, accordingly, be reversed and the case remanded for further proceedings not inconsistent with this opinion."

The U.S. Supreme Court Justices argued that Mr. Pickering had not been malicious in his criticism of the school board. He had merely attempted to point out why the public was reluctant to support additional tax measures, given the board's past performance in allocating funds. The U.S. Supreme Court did point out the need for teachers to vent their personal frustration about a board member or superintendent in private, but if their criticism is of the group, and their facts are substantially correct, they are within their free speech rights to air thoughts publicly. The impact of this landmark is that teachers do not leave their constitutional rights at the door of the schoolhouse.

In the case of *Belyeu v. Coosa County Board of Education* 998 F.2d 925 (1993), a teacher made public comments on racial curriculum issues. Belyeu was a special education teacher aide for the Coosa County School System, and she had a daughter enrolled in the school system's high school. During the meeting of the high school Parent Teacher Association (PTA), the aide said the school should adopt a program to commemorate Black History month. Belyeu said white students should be taught about black historical figures as a compulsory part of the curriculum, just as black students are taught about white historical figures. Immediately after the meeting, the Principal asked to speak with her and told her he wished she had raised this issue privately rather than publicly. The aide was not rehired for the following school year and she sued contending she was not rehired because of her public speech, and failure to rehire her violated her right to speak on matters of public concern. A trial court ruled in the school district's favor on the grounds that the school district's interest in avoiding racial tension outweighed the aide's rights to free speech.

On appeal, however, the Eleventh Circuit reversed, writing that the aide's "remarks did not disrupt the school system's function by enhancing racial division, nor, based on the nature or context of her remarks, was her speech likely to raise racial tensions. For now, the courts must balance the public school teacher's interest in commenting upon a matter of public concern against the school officials' interest in promoting an efficient workplace of public service.

CASE STUDIES

I. Student marked unexcused

Billy was in history class learning about the Christian Crusades in the Middle East. Being an avid Christian he was offended by the facts and got up and left class. The teacher penalized him by marking him unexcused. Billy's parents called the Principal and claimed the teacher violated his right to religious excusal.

1. Was Billy's right to religious excusal violated?

2. Was the teacher right to mark Billy unexcused?

II. Group denied graduation ceremony in gym

The Board has allowed different groups of people to use the gym as long as the instructional periods of the school are not impaired. A group of graduating students at a private high school, and their parents, decided to have a private baccalaureate ceremony in the gym. They got verbal permission to use the gym. The Board consulted the School District Attorney for an opinion on whether the private ceremony should be allowed on school grounds. The School District Attorney's office said it should not be allowed because prayers might be offered at the ceremony. The Board agreed with the School Attorney.

1. Is the Board decision rational? *no, because there was a preveous equal access of the gym.*

2. What do you think is at stake in this scenario?

3. What do you think of the Attorney General's response?

III. School encouraging religion

Jill was passing out Bibles in the halls during school time. Mohamed, a Muslim, accepted the free Bible and brought it home. His parents called the school and claimed the school was accepting Christianity by allowing the students to pass out the Bible, therefore offending Mohamed's religious freedom.

1. How would you respond to the parent's complaint?

IV. Students argue right to protect homosexual

The school district adopted an anti-harassment policy intended to provide a safe school environment for students. The policy defined harassment as verbal or physical conduct based on one's perceived race, religion, color, national origin, gender, sexual orientation, disability, or other personal characteristics, and which has the purpose or effect of substantially interfering with a student's educational performance or creating an intimidating, hostile or offensive environment. A group of students sued, alleging that the policy violated the Free Speech Clause of the First Amendment. They felt obligated by their religion to speak out on issues of morality (School Law Bulletin).

1. Was this policy unconstitutional under the First Amendment?

Because the policy is so broad, it's unconstitutional. (IV)

2. Do Christians have the right to speak against homosexuals? *yes*

3. Should the students have been punished for speaking out about their religious beliefs?

4. Would you consider this policy to be very broad?

V. Parent compliant about student unjustly punished

Ivan wore a "Satan Is My Friend" shirt to class one day. Mrs. Wilson, his teacher, was offended by the un-Christian message. She told him to turn his shirt inside out. Ivan refused. She proceeded to give him a Saturday work crew assignment under the penalty of lack of taste that the shirt displayed. His dad later called the school saying Ivan was punished unjustly because the school dress code only prohibits offensive clothing.

1. Was Ivan punished unjustly? *If there is no policy against his type of clothing, then he can wear it.*

2. Was Mrs. Wilson going to be offended if the statement was "Jesus Is My Friend?

3. How would you handle the situation? *what is the school policy? Every school has a dress code.*

VI. *McCollum v. Board of Education*, 333 U.S. 203 (1948).

An Illinois school board permitted representatives of several religions to teach religion classes to those students in grades four through nine whose parents signed cards indicating that they wanted them to attend. The classes were held during school hours and inside the school building. Students who attended the classes were excused from their secular schedule for that period of time. Other students remained in their regular classes. In this case, taxpayers challenged the constitutionality of the program.

1. What do you think about the Board's decision?

2. Did this decision meet the two-part test standard?

3. Did attendance to religious classes conflict with the compulsory attendance law?

VII. *Wisconsin v. Yoder*, 406 U.S. 205 (1972).

Members of the Old Order Amish religious community, a Christian sect that has been a distinct and identifiable group for three centuries, were convicted of violating Wisconsin's compulsory school attendance law. The law required parents to send their children to school until age sixteen. The Amish refused to send their children to any formal school, public or private, beyond the 8th grade because they believed that further formal education would seriously impede their children's preparation for adult life and for religious practice within the Amish communities. The Amish did provide their teenagers with substantial practical training at home for Amish adulthood. Further, it was shown that the children would most likely be self-sufficient citizens. The Amish challenged the constitutionality of the school attendance law as it applied to them.

1. Could "parens patriea" override parents' rights? ~guardian~

2. Which Amendment will the court use to rule on this case? ~The State is the guardian of all Minors~

3. Could compulsory attendance beyond 8th grade have detrimental effects on the Amish?

1. NO

2. 14th & 1st

3. Yes

Chapter

3

DUE PROCESS

"Due process is defined as a course of legal proceedings established by the legal system of a nation to protect individual rights and liberty" (Encarta (1997)). It is best defined in one word: fairness. Throughout United States history, its Constitution, statutes, and case laws have provided standards for the fair treatment of citizens. This standard is known as due process. When students or teachers are treated unfairly by school officials or the government, they are said to have been deprived of, or denied, due process.

Procedural due process of the law refers to the fair procedure which must be followed when a citizen's rights are to be infringed upon by a government agent. The constitution protects the rights of individuals (including children) against an infringement of life, liberty or property without fair government procedures. "Government takes many actions that may deprive people of life, liberty, or property. In each case, some form of due process is required. For example, a state might fire someone from a government job, revoke a prisoner's parole, or cut off someone's social security payments. Due process does not prohibit these actions, but it does require that certain procedures be followed before any action is taken" (Street Law, p. 486).

The phrase "due process of law", when applied to substantive rights, means that the state is without power to deprive a person of life, liberty or property by an act having no reasonable relation to any proper governmental purpose, or which is so far beyond the necessity of the case as to be an arbitrary exercise of governmental power.

Substantive due process may be implicated by the rules written by educators to control student behavior, such as the student handbook. For example, in the case of *Goss v. Lopez*, 419 U.S. 565, 1975, students brought a class action against appellant school officials seeking a declaration that the Ohio statute permitting suspensions without due process was unconstitutional and an order enjoining the officials to remove the references to the suspensions from the students' records. The class action also sought to enjoin school officials from issuing future suspensions without due process hearings. Did Ohio school officials have the right to suspend students from school without a hearing of any kind and in the process violate their procedural due process component of the Fourteenth Amendment?

In this case nine public high school students in Columbus, Ohio, were suspended for up to 10 days from school for misconduct for various activities connected with widespread student unrest. Six of the named plaintiffs, Rudolph Sutton, Tyrone Washington, Susan Cooper, Deborah Fox, Clarence Byars, and Bruce Harris were students at the Marion-Franklin High School and were each suspended due to disruptive or disobedient conduct committed in the presence of the school administrator who ordered the suspension. One student, Washington, disrupted a class and was ordered to leave but refused to do so. Sutton, in the presence of the Principal, physically attacked a police officer who was attempting to remove Tyrone Washington from the auditorium. The other four students were suspended for similar conduct. None were given a hearing to determine the operative facts underlying the suspension, but they and their parents were offered the opportunity to attend a conference, subsequent to the effective date of the suspension, to discuss the students' futures.

Lopez was suspended in connection with a disturbance in the lunchroom, which involved some physical damage to school property. Lopez testified that at least 75 other students were suspended from his school on the same day. He also testified that he was not a party to the destructive conduct, but was instead an innocent bystander. Crome was present at a demonstration at a high school other than the one she was attending. There, she was arrested together with others, taken to the police station and released without being formally charged. Before she went to school on the following day she was notified that she had been suspended for a 10-day period. The appellant argued that there is no constitutional right to an education at public expense; the due process does not protect against expulsions from the public school system. The Fourteenth Amendment forbids the state to deprive any person of life, liberty, or property without due process of law. The U.S. District Court declared that the students were denied due process of law in violation of the Fourteenth Amendment because they were "suspended without a hearing prior to the suspension or within a reasonable time thereafter," that the statute and implementing regulations were unconstitutional, and granted the injunction. The U.S. District Court for the Southern District of Ohio found for the students and the U. S. Supreme Court affirmed the decision.

Reasoning: Students facing suspension from a public school have property and liberty interests that qualify for protection under the Due Process Clause of the Fourteenth Amendment. Once Ohio afforded the right to an education to the people of the appellees' class they could no longer withdraw that right on the grounds of misconduct without fundamentally fair procedures to determine if the misconduct did occur. Students do not shed their constitutional rights at the schoolhouse door (*Tinker vs. Des Moines*, 1969). A student has a legitimate right to a public education as a property interest protected by the Due Process Clause that may not be taken away without observing minimal protections. Since a suspension, if sustained and recorded, could have severe damage to a student's reputation and future employment, when the state claimed the right to determine unilaterally and without process that misconduct had occurred, the state collided with the Due Process Clause prohibition against arbitrary deprivation of liberty. Additionally, a ten-day suspension is not a minimal punishment and may not be imposed without regard to the Due Process Clause. Neither the property interest in educational benefits temporarily denied, nor liberty interest in reputation is so insubstantial that suspensions may constitutionally be imposed by any method the school chooses. The court ruled that in cases of suspensions of 10 days or less, students should receive at least: (1) oral or written notice of the charges, and if the student denies the charges, then; (2) a summary of the evidence against the student; and (3) an informal opportunity to present his or her side of the story. Justice White's opinion specifically did not require that hearings in connection with short suspensions must afford the student the right to a lawyer, to confront and to cross-examine witnesses against the student, or to call his or her own witnesses to verify the student's version of the incident.

THE ELEMENTS OF SUBSTANTIVE DUE PROCESS

In order to avoid some of the conflicts that may occur during the implementation of rules in the school or classroom, the following factors must be considered:

1. Reasonableness: Schools are always bound by the requirement that their rules and regulations are reasonable (*Burnside v. Byars*, 363 .2D.777 (1966)).

2. Proportionality: Schools are responsible for ascertaining that punishment given to a student for violation of a reasonable rule is proportional to the transgression (*Lee v. Macon County Board of Education*, 190F. Supp. 307 (1972)).

3. Fair warning: Students have the constitutional right to be guided by rules that are specific enough so an ordinary person can know and do what is expected.

4. Equal application: The equal application requirement sets limits on the discretion of school officials to single out individuals for treatment that is applied to others.

5. Equal protection: Equal protection from state police power is also guaranteed by the Fourteenth Amendment (adapted from my class notes).

As Supreme Court Justice Foster, delivering the landmark case *Tinker v. Des Moines*, 393.U.S 503. (1969) decision stated, "It can be argued that neither students nor teachers shed their constitutional rights at the school house door."

There are some sensitive areas of equal protection concerning discrimination that teachers should take into consideration. For example, race, gender, and unequal treatment of boys and girls must be avoided by all means. Special attention must be given to equal treatment for the poor, underprivileged, and politically powerless students as compared to consideration for all others.

The Fifth Amendment to the United States Constitution states that "no person shall be deprived of life, liberty, or property, without due process of the law." Likewise, the Fourteenth Amendment to the Constitution prohibits the states from depriving any person of life, liberty or property without due process of the law, nor can a state deny any person within its jurisdiction the equal protection of the laws. The due process procedures required in specific situations depend on several factors: (1) the seriousness of the harm that might be done to the citizen; (2) the cost to the government, in time and money, of carrying out the procedures; (3) the risk of making an error without the procedure (Street Law, p.485).

A few years ago, decisions for suspension or expulsion of students were made easily on the notion that "to attend public schools was a privilege which could be taken away…" Students who broke the rules were suspended from school without an opportunity to present their sides of the story. The decisions in the cases of *Tinker v. Des Moines* and *Goss v. Lopez* demonstrate that school children are "persons" under the Constitution and are therefore entitled to a developing set of procedural and substantive due process protections.

To suspend a student from school for a brief period of time can have an adverse effect on the child's education and liberty interests and constitutes a deprivation which requires due process of the law. If a person/ student has a right to due process, certain procedures must be followed before any right is taken away. These procedures are:

1. A clear written statement of charges;

2. A right to be represented by counsel and to be informed of this fact;

3. A reasonable period of time for preparation of a defense;

4. The right to confront and cross-examine witnesses in most situations;

5. The right to a hearing before an impartial tribunal.

Goss provides a good opportunity to emphasize both the flexible nature of due process and the importance of fair procedure in avoiding errors. Students have the right to be informed of the charges brought against them and must be given an opportunity to be heard.

In regard to teachers' rights, McCarthy and Cambron put forth some guidelines to be followed:

1. A teacher is entitled to due process of the law prior to dismissal when property or liberty interests exist. Property interest is created through tenure, implied tenure, or contract.

2. A liberty interest may arise if the dismissal action imposes a stigma or damage on the teacher's reputation.

3. At minimum, due process requires that teachers be provided with notice specifying reasons for dismissal and an opportunity for a hearing at which they can present evidence and confront witnesses.

4. All procedures specified by statute or contract must be followed in the dismissal process (adapted from my class notes).

In reference to student discipline in school, "The Fifth and Fourteenth Amendments to the United States Constitution prohibit the states from depriving any person of life, liberty, or property without due process of the law." Long suspension from school can have an adverse impact on the interests of the student. As a rule of thumb, if parents want to contest a suspension, the kind of hearing available matches the severity of the disciplinary action. The longer the suspension, the more process that is due.

FERPA—General Guideline for Students

Historically, federal mandates on students' educational and personal records were sparse. But Senator James Buckley, a parent of six children, wanted students' educational records to be protected. A number of national educational issues led him to believe that there was growing evidence of the abuse of student records. Senator Buckley believed that protection of individual privacy is vital to the existence of a free society; that is, all people have a right to privacy of records. In fair information practices, students should be able to know, review, and challenge information kept by institutions. This includes basic rights to due process (McDonald, 1999).

In August of 1974, President Ford signed Public Law (P.L.) 93-380, and when James L. Buckley from New York spoke to the Legislative Conference of the National Congress of Parents and Teachers on March 12, 1975, he affirmed his desire to assure the Family Education Rights and Privacy Act (McDonald, 1999). Known as the Buckley Amendment, this privacy act made an astounding mark on legislation for students' rights in schools and institutions that receive federal assistance. It is still one of the main sources of legislation that protects children's rights to privacy (educational records) (U.S. Department of Education, 2003).

The Act defines educational records as "those records, files, documents, and other materials" that pertain information about a student and are "maintained by an educational agency or institution" (U.S. Department of Education, 2003). Exceptions include records in the sole possession of personnel or law enforcement, and health treatment records (U.S. Department of Education, 2003). Educational records are information that students may obtain in handwritten, print, computer, media, video, audiotape, film, microfilm, or microfiche form (Raskins, 2003). Educational records may consist of grades, assessments, Individualized Education Plans (IEPs), disciplinary records, health documents, social security numbers, attendance, pictures, or personal information. These and other such documents cannot be released to the public (Council of Chief State School Officers, 1997). Agencies or institutions which do not follow these federal mandates may be denied federal allocation of funds.

Parents, regardless of family circumstances, must consent to any release of their child's personal documents. One or both parents must be included, unless the agency or institution has been provided with a legally binding document that specifically revokes these rights. Once the student reaches the age of majority (18 in Washington State) privacy rights transfer from the parents to the eligible students. Then students may act on their own behalves for the release of their records (U.S. Department of Education, 2003).

The Family Education Right Privacy Act gives the rights to the parent or eligible student to review or confirm the accuracy of the student's educational records. Under FERPA, each agency or institution must provide an annual notification of rights. "The annual report must state to the consented persons that they have a right to inspect and review the student's educational records, to seek changes to the student's records that the parent or eligible student believes to be inaccurate or in violation of the student's privacy right to consent to disclosures of personally identifiable information, and to file a complaint. It shall also include procedures for reviewing documents and requesting amendments of records. All documents must be given in the parents' primary language (U.S. Department of Education, 2003)."

If a school district has a policy of disclosing its records, then it must specify the purpose and procedures for doing so. For example, directory information may be excluded under the FERPA. This information includes name, address, telephone listing, date and place of birth, attendance, major field of study, participation in activities and sports, weight and height, and most recent educational institution attended that may be made into a public document (Council of Chief State School Officers, 1997). Parents are informed of their legal rights under the annual procedures and if they choose not to participate in the directory, they may request in writing to have their information withheld. The No Child Left Behind Act, P.L. 107-110, addressed a disclosure to military recruiters. It is a Federal mandate that schools give information to military recruiters, for recruiting purposes, to the military (U.S. Department of Education, 2003).

Educational records that are kept by the institution or agency must have documentation of all individuals, agencies, or organizations that have requested or obtained access to a student's educational records and the specific interest in obtaining these records. The record of access is available to only the parents and school officials who obtain the files. On

August 6, 1979, Congress stated that FERPA does not prohibit state and local educational officials from having access to student or other records. This access may be necessary to insure that federal or state legal requirements are met. The following are parties allowed to access student's records (Department of Education, 2003):

▼ School officials with legitimate educational interest

▼ Schools to which the student is transferring

▼ Specified officials for audit or evaluation purposes

▼ Parties in connection to financial aid

▼ Organizations conducting certain studies on behalf of the school

▼ Accrediting organizations

▼ Court orders or subpoenas

▼ Appropriate officials in cases of health or safety issues

▼ Juvenile justice system state and local authorities

The privacy laws enacted in 1974 under Senator Buckley have had major impacts on students' rights to privacy.

PEER GRADING

Owasso Independent School District No. I – 011 v. Falvo, Cite as 534 U.S. (2002).

Teachers on many occasions have students score each other's papers as the teacher explains the assignment and read out the correct answers to the class. Parents of one minor claimed that such "peer grading" violates the Family Educational Rights and Privacy Act of 1974 (Buckley Amendment) and filed an action against the school district in the District Court. In granting petitioners summary judgment, the District Court held that grades put on papers by another student are not educational records. The Tenth Circuit Court reversed the decision stating that "grades marked by students on each other's work are educational records, so the very act of grading is an impermissible release of information to the student grader" (p. 1). The case was argued in November 27, 2001 and decided February 19, 2002.

The finding "No Violation of the Act" was handed down. Justice Scalia, in part, concurring in the judgment said "I agree with the Court that peer-graded student papers do not constitute educational records while they remain in the possession of the peer grader because, as the Court explains, a student who grades another's work is not a person acting for the school in the ordinary meaning of that phrase."

School Discipline

In the 23rd Gallup Poll conducted in 1991, discipline in our public schools was ranked at the top among concerns pertaining to our schools. One of the concerns that everyone involved with the public school system has is the issue of student constitutional rights when it comes to administering discipline. Research states that there are many states in the U.S. that allow teachers and administrators to use physical force while conducting an educational program for the purpose of restraining unruly students or correcting unacceptable behavior. La Morte (1996) labeled this type of discipline as corporal punishment. School districts have the authority to exclude students from school and school activities as a way to control student behavior. La Morte referred to this type of discipline as either suspension or expulsion. The traditional type of disciplines have been the subject of much controversy in our society lately, so it is worth taking a look at other proposed methods of punishment as an alternative to corporal punishment or suspension.

When schools are dealing with the issue of discipline, they interplay with the constitutional rights of the individual student. Students have rights under the Constitution of the United States. Although these rights may be somewhat limited within the school system, the student has a property and liberty interest in education.

Under the Fourteenth Amendment, students have the right to due process. Within the public school system, students have the right to be told what infringement they have committed, have an explanation of the punishment, an explanation of the evidence, and an opportunity to explain themselves. And any short or long term suspension requires a note to parents explaining the length of suspension and information about grievance procedures.

Students have the right to freedom of expression under the First Amendment. This was established in the 1969 case of *Tinker v. Des Moines* and has continued since then with a variety of other cases such as *Bethel School District v. Fraser 1986*, and *Stephenson v. Davenport Community School District 1997*. These cases established that if a student's expression has the potential to bring harm to other students or to property, then the school has the right to limit that freedom.

Parents, as the legal representative and guardian of their children, have rights to know about the learning environments of their children. It is a common understanding that parents should be involved in every step of their child's education, which includes discipline, if needed. They, like their children, have the right to know that their child is being treated fairly, is free from harm, and that they have legal recourse if these rights are not being met. What teachers should keep in mind, according to Robert E. Rubinstein in Hints for Teaching Success in Middle School, is that parents want to see and feel that school people care for their children and care about their children's personal happiness and success. Parents need our support and our help in any way possible to help their children succeed. Since teachers and parents have a student's best interest in mind, we can consult each other for guidance.

Many books have been written on the issue of student discipline and credible publications cite preventative classroom management as a teacher's best way to ensure that everyone is treated justifiably within the classroom. A few of the preventative techniques include; posting clear, concise rules within the classroom, having a neat organized classroom to avoid accidents, being consistent with rules and expectations of student behavior, and being organized as a teacher.

In "Hints for Teaching Success in Middle School", the *Teacher Ideas Press* writes: "You cannot control students' behaviors, their desires to learn, or their success in learning. All you can do is control yourself; model with your own behavior, desire to learn, and demonstrate willingness to help students learn. Teachers need to be constantly aware of these limitations."

Teachers have the power to discipline students in the classroom. Teachers are empowered to remove a student under their immediate supervision from the classroom for disruption. Students removed by the teacher may not return to the classroom without the teacher's approval. Teachers may use assertive discipline to maximize their potential to meet the needs of a class, but must in no way violate the best interests of the students. A teacher should document everything including contact with parents, discipline problems and contact with the Principal. In doing so, they are creating a record of student behavior that may be needed to defend the school district's action or themselves.

CORPORAL PUNISHMENT IN SCHOOL

La Morte (1996) defines corporal punishment "as the use of such physical contact as striking, paddling, or spanking of a student by an educator" (p. 129). Yudof, Kirp, and Levin (1992) observed that corporal punishment has been in American schools since the colonial period. They note that despite the abandonment of this method for disciplining criminal offenders and the transformation from the reliance on private schooling to the public school systems, this practice continues to be used to correct deviant behavior in many public schools across the country. They also state that opinions have been divided regarding this type of punishment for more than a century. Despite this controversy, it is clear that where state laws permit it, the courts will uphold the practice with reasonable application and have determined that such discipline does not violate a student's right to due process. As Justice Powell wrote in delivering the Court's opinion in the pivotal case, *Ingram vs. Wright* (1977): "We are reviewing here a legislative judgment, rooted in history and reaffirmed in the laws of many States that corporal punishment serves important educational interests. This judgment must be viewed in light of the disciplinary problems commonplace in the schools"(p. 133). In the case of *Ingram vs. Wright* (1977) the parents sued their school district on the grounds that the paddling of their children, which caused one child to suffer serious injury and another to miss eleven days of school, was cruel and unusual punishment and therefore a violation of the Eighth Amendment. The Eighth Amendment of the United States Constitution states that excessive bail shall not be required, nor excessive fines imposed, nor cruel and unusual punishments inflicted. According to Alexander & Alexander (1999) the Court ruled that the prohibition against cruel and unusual punishment was intended to protect those who had been convicted of a crime, and did not apply to a student's paddling at school. Kern and David Alexander noted that the Eighth Amendment was intended for three things: "to limit the types of punishment on criminals, to provide against grossly disproportionate punishment, and to limit what is to be punished as a crime. In light of this, they state that it is "difficult to conceive of corporal punishment as being within the scope of the Eighth Amendment" (p. 318). The Court was reasoning that school children needed less protection than convicted criminals because of the openness of the school system and its surveillance by the community. Once again Mr. Justice Powell summed up the opinion of the Court in the Ingram case by saying that in view of the low incidence of abuse, the openness of schools, and the common law safeguards that already existed, the risk of error that might result in violation of a schoolchild's substantive rights could only be regarded as minimal. When examining the Wright case, Michael La Morte observed that corporal punishment was not only challenged as unconstitutional under the Eighth Amendment but under the Fourteenth Amendment as well. According to Mark Yudof, et al. two things must be looked at when examining this Amendment. First are the individual's interests included under the protection of life, liberty, or property, and second are the procedures needed to constitute due process of the law. Valente & Valente (1998) state that the Supreme Court decided that corporal punishment could be carried out without a hearing because the child's property right to free education was not affected by the punishment. Furthermore, the student's liberty interests were not violated in light of the fact that they were outweighed by the school's and state's interests in effective and prompt discipline and are protected by state tort law. Justice Powell concluded that because the practice is limited and authorized by common law, the Due Process Clause does not require that a hearing be conducted or a notice be sent before the implementation of corporal punishment.

The Supreme Court has established that teachers may, as state law allows, administer corporal punishment as an extension of their "in loco perentis" authority. Data Research and Valente & Valente both note that the first consideration in administering corporal punishment is whether or not the discipline is reasonable. Though there are no set guidelines, there are many considerations when judging reasonableness, such as: the nature of the student's conduct and apparent motive; the student's age, sex, mental and physical condition; the student's past disciplinary record; whether force was necessary and appropriate; and whether or not this punishment was particularly degrading or conducted in a degrading manner.

In Thomas McDaniel's article "The Teacher's Ten Commandments: School Law in the Classroom," he sets forth five considerations for using corporal punishment. First, "the punishment must never lead to permanent injury" (p. 3). Valente & Valente note that while discipline that produces minor bruises and pain will not likely be considered excessive, any punishment that produces bleeding, sprains, deep bruises and fractures will. Second, McDaniel warns that the punishment can't be used to enforce an unreasonable rule. Third, "the punishment must not be motivated by spite, malice, or revenge" (p. 3). The Supreme Court of Oklahoma found a superintendent in violation of the reasonableness standard when he beat a child "in a state of intoxicated rage" (p. 307), causing the boy to need medical treatment. While McDaniel notes that a teacher may use all the force necessary to protect himself as well as other teachers and students, a teacher was held liable by the Court of Appeal of Louisiana in a case in which a 14-year-old boy hit the teacher and then snapped a rubber band into the teacher's face and then fled into a classroom. The teacher pulled the child from the class about ten minutes later, took him to a vacant room, and punched the student several times. Fourth, "the punishment must not ignore such variables as the student's age, sex, size, and physical condition" (p.3). Fifth, the punishment must be administered to appropriate parts of the body and with appropriate instruments. Valente & Valente state that courts have disapproved of such instruments as broken paddles and cattle prods for employing punishment. A teacher in Texas was held liable for cuffing an eight-year-old boy in the ear. The judge noted in his decision that, "Nature has provided a part of the anatomy for chastisement, and tradition holds that such chastisement should there be applied" (p.3).

It is important to note once again that teachers and school administrators may inflict corporal punishment only in the absence of state legislation to the contrary. La Morte observes that the states of Alaska, California, Connecticut, Hawaii, Illinois, Iowa, Maine, Maryland, Massachusetts, Michigan, Minnesota, Montana, Nebraska, Nevada, New Hampshire, New Jersey, New York, North Dakota, Oregon, Utah, Vermont, Washington, and Wisconsin all have laws prohibiting the use of corporal punishment in schools. He also notes that in the state of Rhode Island all local school boards have prohibited this disciplinary practice. In the states that do allow for this type of punishment, further restrictions are imposed such as requiring permission from the parents or school administrators. According to Valente & Valente the Principal or Superintendent would be the only one allowed to administer the spanking, or the parent's permission must be obtained before the discipline could take place.

SUSPENSION: IN-SCHOOL AND OUT-OF-SCHOOL

Suspension is a form of discipline often used in schools. This form of discipline is popular because the disruptive students are removed from the classroom, thus allowing the teacher and other students to continue without disruption. The National School Board's Association says, "suspended students lose valuable instruction and are likely to distrust the authority that has rejected them. Suspension rewards teachers and others for avoiding classroom responsibilities. Suspended students are usually the very students who most need direct instruction" (p. 61). Suspension may be the ideal action in the eyes of teachers, administrators, and even other students, but students who are suspended have a property right to an education.

When students are at risk of harming themselves or others, and there is no other alternative, suspension can be considered an option. Price and others state that since suspension should only be used in emergency cases it should last no longer than a day. Suspension should last only as long as the emergency. Of course this is not always the case. Often students are removed from the classroom and suspended multiple times. According to some educators, a major flaw in suspension is that the students who are most often suspended are the students who have no interest in school to begin with, so they see suspension as a reward, not a punishment.

For example, in Washington State, Revised Code of Washington 28A.600.410 states that school districts are encouraged to find alternatives to suspension including reducing the length of a student's suspension conditioned by the commencement of counseling or other treatment services. This law is to protect students from multiple suspensions for exorbitant lengths of time. Also included in this Revised Code of Washington is the condition that schools are not required to pay for counseling or other treatment services, except for those that were agreed upon by the school district in making suspension decisions. Counseling is one option to suspension, but another option is in-school suspension.

In-school suspension is an option to suspension that allows a student to stay in the school, but instead of participating in the actual classroom setting, the student is separated from other students. In-school suspension is seen as the ideal punishment in the eyes of many people since the students' property right to education is not taken away. The student is in school, being offered an education, but removed from the classroom setting where he or she could be disruptive to others. Although in-school suspension may seem like the perfect answer to the controversy of removing students from the school, there are still people who believe that it is unjust to seclude students from the rest of the school. In schools, it often becomes common knowledge which students are in in-school suspension, and this affects the liberty rights of students since their reputations will often times be tainted. Since I have discussed the issues of in-school suspension, the author would like to shed some light on school expulsion.

Expulsion shares many of its definitions with suspension; it is simply a more severe measure in dealing with discipline. Expulsion is an extended suspension. It tends to be for long periods of time, such as the remainder of the term or school year. While suspension may be given for offenses of a lesser degree, like cheating, fighting, or smoking, expulsion is reserved for extreme cases dealing with endangering others, for example using drugs or carrying weapons on school grounds.

Expulsion follows the same due process laws as suspension, meaning students have to be notified and given a hearing so that they may state their side. According to Washington State RCW 28A.600.020, a Principal shall consider imposing long-term suspension or expulsion as a sanction when deciding appropriate disciplinary action for a student who (a) engages in two or more violations within a three-year period, and (b) engages in one or more of the offenses listed in RCW 13.04.155.

When a student is expelled from school, the school district is required to provide the student with an alternate education program. This can be anything from providing work for the student for home-schooling, to sending the student to another school or school district. Students can not simply be expelled without any alternatives for an education. This protects both the student and their Fourteenth Amendment rights.

Student discipline lies in the hands of teachers and administrators. While teachers are often the primary disciplinarians in the classroom and school setting, when problems arise that cannot be settled in a timely manner within the classroom, students are referred to the principal, or superintendent. Price et al. state, in general, the rule is that the more serious the punishment, the higher the authority required to impose it.

Students are most often referred to the administration when their actions require suspension or expulsion. In most states it is not within the teacher's jurisdiction to suspend students. In most states only a principal, superintendent, or school board can suspend a student. Teachers are responsible for minor discipline problems in the classroom. Each classroom has a set of rules that govern that class. When rules are broken, the teacher is responsible for administering consequences.

EXCLUSION FROM EXTRACURRICULAR ACTIVITIES

Students can be deprived of extracurricular activities without suspension from school. Most often students are suspended from all school activities at one time. Not often is it seen that students are suspended from extracurricular activities without suspension from school also. If a student's behavior is severe enough to be suspended from one, he/she will commonly be suspended from both.

Students can only be deprived of participation in an activity if the activity is a school function. After hours and off-campus activities, which are not school related, cannot be punishable by the school. Courts have begun to recognize that extracurricular activities are generally a fundamental part of the school's educational program. To be denied the opportunity to participate in these activities can be as serious a loss of the right to an education as a suspension is.

When students are suspended from extracurricular activities they are also entitled to due process. Suspension from extracurricular activities, similar to suspension from school, requires the student to be notified of the suspension. The student is entitled to an informal hearing where the student's voice can be heard. Students have the right to due process whenever they are withheld from a school function.

As stated in the introduction, discipline in our public schools has been ranked at the top among the concerns in our schools for many years according to the 23rd Gallup Poll in 1991, yet school officials and teachers are at a loss as to what to do about this problem. Since traditionally accepted methods such as corporal punishment, suspension and expulsion have become taboos to some extent, school officials have been forced to come up with alternative methods for discipline.

In an attempt to find an answer to discipline problems in our public schools, a few principals have begun instituting Saturday school. This punishment requires students to appear at school on Saturday morning and remain there until Saturday afternoon. They participate in activities ranging from physical labor to reflective writing regarding the reason they are in Saturday school and what they could do to avoid its occurrence. Students are normally assigned Saturday school by the Principal, not by the classroom teacher, and a letter is sent home prior to Saturday so that arrangement with parents can be made to ensure student attendance.

According to a study done by John Winborn, Saturday school may not only appear to be an acceptable alternative to solving disciplinary problems, it may also be looked upon as a step toward development and adoption of disciplinary methods that foster internal rather than external control of students. The discussion on discipline is to empower schools to develop alternative means to handle student problems, and administrators and teachers must now be resourceful and creative in their approaches to solving this problem.

ZERO TOLERANCE

Over the past decade school violence began to rise in numbers. This rise in violent crimes caught the attention of the nation. Seeking to stop these crimes, a zero tolerance policy came into affect. Although the zero tolerance policy has had the most attention in schools, it originated in the military.

A zero tolerance policy came into affect as early as 1983, from state and federal drug enforcement policies. The first case where the policy was used began in the military. The Navy reassigned 40 crewmembers because of suspected drug use. A couple of years later, a U.S. attorney in San Diego, California, used the phrase as the title to a program he was developing to prevent drug smuggling. This program made it so that any sea craft found with drugs could be impounded. The quantity of the drug found did not matter. Within two years this program began to receive national attention, and since the program was working so well, it was changed to include anyone crossing the border with even trace amounts of drugs. This made it possible for law enforcement to impound cars and trucks in addition to the boats already seized. The program continued to gain national attention. The term "zero tolerance" then began to be used for many different behaviors, including everything from environmental pollution to skateboarding, and sexual harassment to the use of boom boxes.

The original zero tolerance program began to fade out in the late 1980s, but this was just the beginning for zero tolerance in school settings. In 1989, there were two school districts which adopted the zero tolerance policy. One was in Orange County, California, and the other was in Louisville, Kentucky. Both of these districts used zero tolerance policies to fight drugs and/or gang-related activity. By the early 90s, the policy had worked its way into the New York schools. The superintendent used it to minimize school disruptions. This included a ban on hats, increased use of police power, and suspension for any school disruption. By 1993, zero tolerance was adopted by a majority of the school districts in America. The government further fueled the push for zero tolerance in schools. In 1994, President Clinton signed the Gun Free Schools Act into law. This law made it a mandatory expulsion of one calendar year if a student was caught with a firearm in a school zone. Also, if a school wanted federal funding it was required to enact a zero tolerance policy toward guns.

Even though the zero tolerance policy was mandated to deal with guns, many school districts have extended this scope to include other infractions. These infractions range from violent crimes that occur in the schools, such as murder, suicide, fights, assaults without a weapon, rape or sexual battery, and fights with a weapon, to sexual harassment, robbery, vandalism, theft and larceny, smoking, or using any other type of drugs, including alcohol, and possession of any weapon on school premises (NCES, 1998).

Many parents welcomed these stricter regulations. They hoped enacting the policies would give principals and school board members more leeway to punish the violators, and this in turn would lower the violent acts on the rise in American schools. But has this theory worked as intended? Let us look at a few of the issues.

CASE STUDIES ON ZERO TOLERANCE

Case 1: Lisa Smith

Lisa Smith was an honor student, a cheerleader, and a student council member at Lakeview Middle School in the Dallas suburbs. She played violin in the school orchestra, won awards at the science fair and had just finished a highly praised project on the Holocaust for an honors history class. But, one mistake later, the eighth-grader who had never known trouble faced five months in a military-style boot camp. Her offense: She violated the school's zero tolerance policy by bringing to school a 20-ounce bottle of cherry 7-Up mixed with a few drops of grain alcohol. Under the school's policy, the school was compelled to give her the "academic death sentence" even if her only other trip to the principal's office was to organize an orchestra fund-raiser, and even if she is, in the words of one teacher, "a sweetheart" (Cauchon, 1999).

1. Is what Lisa Smith did wrong?

2. Does she deserve punishment?

Case 2: Bringing a Knife to School

A 10-year-old at Twin Peaks Charter Academy in Longmont, Colorado, was expelled because her mother had put a small knife in her lunchbox to cut an apple. When the student realized the knife might violate the school's zero tolerance policy, she turned it in to a teacher who told her she did the right thing. Still, the child was expelled. Her expulsion brought national ridicule to the St. Vrain Valley School District.

1. Should the school be ridiculed for expelling the student?

Case 3: Honor Roll Student (Nameless!)

A senior honor role student began to act in a bizarre manner in the cafeteria during lunch one day. He was taken to the nurse who suspected he had taken a hallucinogen. The Dean of Students was called to the scene. The young man admitted that he had bought several LSD tablets at the local mall the night before and had taken one just before lunch. The young man, who up until that point had been a good citizen of the school, was suspended, given a hearing with his parents and district administrators, and required to complete the rest of the school year in the district's alternative education program. He was required to enroll in high school specialty courses delivered by the alternative program and placed among the other students.

1. Was the placement harmful to the student?

2. Are his chances of attending a credible college destroyed?

Case 4: York County

Recently, in a York County school district, a kindergarten boy was suspended for five days because he brought a nail clipper to school, and school officials viewed this item as a weapon. The incident was widely publicized by the local media, and the boy's parents contested the fairness of the suspension, protesting that the boy was deprived of five days of his education and didn't even understand what he had done wrong.

1. Was the suspension fair?
2. What can the schools do to alleviate the problem?

Other cases that serve as prime examples of how a zero tolerance policy can affect an individual include a little boy kissing a girl on the cheek. Although many consider this to be developmentally appropriate for a five-year-old, he was suspended from school. In another case, a male high school student learned that a suicidal friend had a weapon. He persuaded her to give it to him. When he handed it to school authorities, he was expelled (McCune, 2000).

Why did the first student get punished for doing something that is socially acceptable? Why was the second student punished for doing the right thing and helping to save another student's life? The issue of zero tolerance is something you may have to contend with in your classroom.

DRUG TESTING

In the mid 1990s, certain school districts in the United States began implementing programs of random drug testing of students who were not involved in athletics. Generally, such testing programs were a response to a perceived increase in drug use in a particular district's schools, but random testing programs have been the basis of lawsuits brought on behalf of students affected by such programs. The primary issue in all the following cases is one of privacy rights as described in the Fourth Amendment of the United States Constitution. This section will outline three cases, one of which has become a legal standard in education privacy cases.

The case which serves as the basis for later decisions in education privacy rights is *Vernonia School District 47J v. Wayne Acton, et ux., etc.* This case, an appeal by the Vernonia School District of a lower court's ruling, was argued in the U.S. Supreme Court. The facts in the case are straightforward. School personnel in the Vernonia district observed a marked rise in student drug use, with a concurrent increase in disciplinary problems. School officials were concerned because athletes were seen as leaders of the school drug culture and because risk of injury due to drug use, especially while participating in a sporting event, was high.

After soliciting community input, the district School Board designed and implemented a three part random testing policy. Students wishing to participate in school sports were to sign, as must their parents, a consent form agreeing to drug testing. All student athletes were tested via urinalysis at the beginning of the sports season, and after that, 10 percent of the athletes were tested weekly for the duration of the season.

One student and his parents refused to sign the consent forms and instead filed suit seeking declaratory and injunctive relief from enforcement of the drug testing policy. The suit alleged that the testing policy violated both the U.S. Constitution's Fourth Amendment and a provision in the Oregon State Constitution.

The U.S. District Court for the District of Oregon dismissed the plaintiff's suit. The plaintiff appealed and the Ninth Circuit Court of Appeals reversed the lower court decision. The Court of Appeals agreed with the plaintiff's contention that the policy did violate both the U.S. and Oregon Constitutions. At that point, the Vernonia School District requested certiorari from the U.S. Supreme Court. The Court agreed to hear the case and consequently ruled in favor of the district.

The Court ruling was based primarily on interpretation of the Fourth Amendment prohibition against unreasonable search and seizure. The Court found that the final measure in constitutionality of a search is the concept of reasonableness. The reasonableness standard balances the individual's right to privacy against the search that supports legitimate government interests. Under the Fourth Amendment, there has been no minimum of state interest established to guide whether a warrantless search is permitted. Further, a search warrant is not required to establish that a search is reasonable. The Court ruled that students who voluntarily participate in athletics have expectations of infringements upon ordinary rights and privileges. Required medical examinations and communal undress in a locker room are but two reasons the Court gave for decreased student expectations of privacy.

The Court, consistent with the T.L.O. decision, agreed that children do not leave constitutional rights at the schoolhouse gate. However, the nature of those rights is circumscribed by several pertinent concepts. First is the concept of in loco parentis, under which the school assumes parental responsibility for children in school. This includes a responsibility on the school's part to prevent illegal or criminal acts by the student. Additionally, unemancipated minors do not exercise basic rights of self-determination in the most limited sense: the right to move about at will is limited by parents and guardians, and in this case, the school system. Importantly, the Court found the parental power exercised by a school over students is not subject to federal Constitutional constraints.

The Court ruling was far from unanimous, with three Justices expressing dissenting views. For example, Justice O'Connor wrote a dissent in which she expressed concern that all students may be liable for warrantless searches based on blanket suspicion of drug use. She noted that blanket searches were " ... not part of any traditional school function..."

CASE ONE

Todd v. Rush County Schools presents " ... a classic constitutional battle" (p. 5). At issue was whether random drug testing via urinalysis violated the Fourth Amendment right to be free of unreasonable searches and seizures. This case originated in Indiana, and a further issue was whether privacy rights guaranteed under the state's Constitution were violated. The suit resulted when a student was prohibited from participating in extracurricular activities due to his parents' refusal to agree to his being randomly tested for drugs. The boy was a volunteer, videotaping school events. In 1996, the Rush County School Board approved a policy barring students from participating in *any* extracurricular activity, or driving to school, unless the students and their parents or guardians consented to the students undergoing random urinalysis testing. Once consent was obtained, urinalysis testing could occur at any time. Initial tests were performed at no cost to the student.

This school policy was a response to a subjective perception held by the Assistant Superintendent and the Athletic Director that drug use was increasing among students. The perception was not well supported by empirical data. Disciplinary referrals of all types, including drug-related issues, showed no consistent pattern of increase over the period 1992-1996. The district had in place for some time a policy covering students involved in athletics. Students were suspended from participation due to use of alcohol, tobacco, or illegal drugs.

Actual testing was performed in a private setting, the student being allowed sufficient time to produce a sample. Samples were analyzed for amphetamines, barbiturates, cocaine, marijuana, and other illegal drugs. Since certain prescription medications will produce a positive result, a student with a positive test result was immediately re-tested. The testing method accuracy rate was in excess of 95 percent. If a retest showed a positive response, the student and parent/guardian were informed. If a satisfactory explanation was provided, such as prescription medicine use, there was no disciplinary consequence for the student. A positive result and no explanation resulted in the student being barred from extracurricular activity until further tests showed negative responses for drug use.

Decision

In reviewing this case, the U.S. District Court for the Southern District of Indiana looked at the *Vernonia* decision. The random testing program was essentially the same in both cases, the major difference being the provision for testing students involved in all extra curricular activities in the Rush County program. The other significant difference was in the actual level of students' involvement with drugs. In Vernonia the level was substantial and documented; in Rush County the level was significantly less and a matter of perception.

In both cases, the Court found the schools acted in loco parentis. In Vernonia that doctrine was interpreted to mean the schools "act as guardian and tutor to children in [their] care", and the "question is whether the search is one a reasonable guardian ... might undertake" (p.7). That ruling was the basis for the decision in Todd. As to the privacy issues raised in Todd, the Court ruled that students' involvements in extracurricular activities are voluntary and a privilege; therefore, students in those activities are liable to regulation beyond the uninvolved student.

The District Court ruled in favor of the school district, finding Todd in all essentials the same as Vernonia. Todd was appealed to the U.S. Court of Appeals for the Seventh Circuit by the plaintiffs. The Circuit Court ruling was affirmed. The plaintiffs then petitioned for a rehearing by the appellate court. The petition was denied. The final step by the plaintiffs was to petition the U.S. Supreme Court for a writ of certiorari to the appeals court. The Supreme Court declined to issue the writ, effectively ending the case in favor of Rush County Schools. Interestingly, the Seventh Circuit Court, in a later ruling, cautioned against interpreting Todd too broadly. The court warned that schools seemed to be testing the limits of recent case law in an effort to allow unsuspicious, random testing of all students.

Case Two

Case two is in most respects similar to Todd. As in Todd, the school district rationale for instituting a testing policy was to prevent possible adverse consequences for individual students who used drugs. Two sisters, (the Linkes), in order to participate in extracurricular activities, signed drug testing consent forms. The plaintiffs filed suit in trial court seeking injunctive and declamatory relief from the drug policy. The suit alleged the testing policy violated the Fourth Amendment of the U.S. Constitution as well as Article 1, Sections 11 and 23 of the Indiana Constitution. These sections prohibit unreasonable searches. Part of the trial court's decision rested on the "special needs" doctrine. The legal concept of special need is used when the governmental body demonstrates that normal processes (i.e., a warrant or probable cause) pursuant to a search would impede or frustrate the timeliness of a search. The doctrine was demonstrated in the U.S. Supreme Court ruling in *New Jersey v. T. L. O.* In that case, obtaining a warrant to search a student's purse would have interfered with the rapid disciplinary procedures needed in schools. The Court ruled that to maintain order in schools, the level of suspicion was diminished in school searches based on probable cause. In this instance, due in large part to the special needs doctrine, the trial court found in favor of the defendants. The plaintiffs appealed the decision to the Court of Appeals of Indiana, Fifth District. The appellate court reversed the trial court's decision and remanded the case back to trial court.

Decision

The appellate court ruled that the Indiana standard for search and seizure was one of reasonableness. Under that concept, unsuspicious testing of students was held to be unconstitutional with regard to the Indiana Constitution. The Judges found that while precedent in Vernonia extended interpretation of situations beyond individual suspicion, there was no need to similarly extend interpretation with regard to the State Constitution. Indeed, the judges saw the school district's implementation of a random testing policy as an "unmistakable move toward randomly testing all students" (Linke).

The Indiana Court of Appeals reversed Linke in favor of the Linkes in August of 2000. It would seem, since the U.S. constitution supersedes any state document, that this case is not yet truly decided. There are numerous rulings by the U.S. Supreme Court that indicate random testing is permissible under the doctrine of in loco parentis. The concept of special needs also comes into play, in that schools need to be able to respond quickly to perceived illegal activities. Justice Scalia, in Vernonia, noted that a balance must be struck between students' privacy interests, the character of the intrusion into that privacy, and the "nature and immediacy" of the school's concern for the well-being of its charges.

Linke v. Northwestern School Corporation (NSC), argued before the Indiana Supreme Court, was decided on March 5, 2002, with three of five Justices agreeing that random drug testing, as executed by NSC, does not constitute an unreasonable search (Supreme Court of Indiana, Supreme Court No. 34S05-0103-CV-151).

Rationale

The high court agreed with NSC that documented rates of drug use in the district's schools could be a legal basis for random drug testing. As in Vernonia, the district had documented evidence of substantially higher rates of drug use among NSC students than average levels found in the state as a whole. That finding gave legitimacy to the development and implementation of a testing policy. NSC contended, and the Court agreed, that the need to combat and deter drug use is a legitimate concern for a school. The Court cited Acton which states that "drug use has an adverse impact on schools' ability to perform their educational mission."

The Linkes argued that unsuspicious search of a student could be likened to an unsuspicious stop of a motorist thought to be in violation of Indiana's mandatory seat-belt law. Law enforcement officers are barred from such a stop. The Linkes contended that the principle is similar in that both situations entail unsuspicious searches. The Linkes argued that, to be reasonable, a search must be based on individualized suspicion.

The Court did not agree. The Court ruled that the two situations are substantively different. The relationship between a law enforcement officer and a supposed criminal is inherently adversarial. Police officials execute duties leading to punitive outcomes for the criminal. In a school setting there is not such an assumed adversarial context. Rather, the Indiana Court cited *New Jersey v. T. L. O.* which claimed that there exists in schools a commonality of interest between students and teachers. Teachers, and by extension, districts under the doctrine of in loco parentis, are charged with the oversight of students' safety.

Privacy interests were a core issue in the case. The Indiana Court examined four areas that relate to student privacy. First, students are not accorded the same privacy interests as adults. In both Acton and T. L. O. the U.S. Supreme court held that minors lack fundamental rights of self-determination. Schools have the authority to supervise and control students to a degree not permitted to adults. The school has a right and responsibility, in matters of discipline, maintained only by parents. The Linkes' contention that students' right of privacy is actually greater than adults was not accepted by the Court. The second point at issue was that of consent. Northwestern School Corporation argued that consent is implied by application to a certain extracurricular activity. The third point extends this concept. Such activities are voluntary, and so students voluntarily waive a certain degree of privacy. Finally, the character of the intrusion was examined to determine if the search was punitive or preventative. Results of NSC tests were not used as a basis for disciplinary measures. The strongest sanction was temporary suspension of a student from the particular activity. Testing was seen as preventative, with a positive test result used as a basis for providing information for counseling the student. In that light, testing could be viewed as part of the school's responsibility to care for its charges.

In deciding the case, the Indiana Court revisited the ruling in *Earls v. Tecumseh*. The district policy of random testing was held to violate the Fourth Amendment prohibition against unreasonable search. In Linke, the Court ruled that NSC had taken care to protect student privacy during sample collection, that there was clear evidence of drug use in the school, and that students were not required to pay any costs associated with the testing program. In deciding Linke, the Indiana Court considered Justice Scalia's test of reasonableness developed for Vernonia. The Court weighed the nature of the intrusion, the privacy issues, and the context of the searches. The Court ruled that the searches were reasonable and that the government, through the school, was acting in the best interests of the students.

As with Vernonia, the district's argument was that students participating in extracurricular activities are representatives of the school. In that light, the school has an interest in regulating behavior of the participants. As noted, the Indiana Supreme Court ruled in favor of Northwestern School Corporation.

Chapter

4

TEACHER-BOARD RELATIONS AND CERTIFICATION

Teacher-board employment relations is a rapidly developing area in school law and one should expect a broad range of employment problems. The ordinary legal issues arising from contracts, salary disputes, tenure, and staff dismissal procedures have been overshadowed recently by those stemming from collective bargaining and negotiations.

In this context, employment relations include contracts of employment, loyalty oaths, teacher tenure laws, dismissal procedures, teacher organization movements, teacher-board bargaining, teacher strikes, sanctions, and other work stoppages. Declining enrollments, reduced tax funds, and reductions in staff positions in many districts have added new and troublesome dimensions to employment relations in public schools.

State laws generally control eligibility for employment as a teacher through certification requirements and procedures. Some states legislate minimum salary schedules, tenure, retirement regulations, and general conditions for hiring. Through legislation, board members are authorized to make employment terms subject to state laws and constitutional limitations. Within the structure of state regulations, local board members are free to develop the teacher employment relations that best serve their district.

All individuals receiving certificates must be of good character, be in good health, and be a citizen of the United States, or legally present an authorized document for employment.

ACADEMIC FREEDOM

What is academic freedom?

Essentially academic freedom is the right of professors, teachers, and students to pursue knowledge and express ideas without interference from their institutions or the state. It is important to note that academic freedom is *not guaranteed* by our Constitution, although the Supreme Court has recognized academic freedom as a First Amendment right. One of the most famous quotes concerning academic freedom came from *Keyishian v. Board of Regents*, 385 U.S. 589 (1967):

> Our Nation is deeply committed to safeguarding academic freedom, which is of transcendent value to all of us and not merely to the teachers concerned. That freedom is therefore a special concern of the First Amendment, which does not tolerate laws that cast a pall of orthodoxy over the classroom. Since the concept of academic freedom arises from the First Amendment, it follows that the principles of academic freedom apply primarily to public institutions, although private institutions may voluntarily adhere to some of the tenets.

Academic freedom was a phrase first discussed in Paris in 1231. Institutions with an autonomous faculty group were formed in Europe and Great Britain in the middle ages, at the start of the 13th century. "Libertas scolastica," or freedom of school (academic freedom), was a consequence of the desire by the university theologian, Thomas Aquinas, and his colleagues, to be separate from church oversight and rule. They fought for the freedom to organize their courses as they saw fit, teach the students of their choice, confer diplomas, and hire professors (Verger, 2001). Schools for the general public existed during this time, primarily to teach the merchant class skills such as arithmetic and sometimes reading, but academic freedom was only a concept applied to the universities, where there was an emphasis on intellectual thought.

Academic freedom was a burgeoning concept until the grip of the Catholic Church on academic life exceeded the ability of intellectuals to keep their freedoms alive. There was an increasing and overwhelming necessity of "ecclesiastical overlay" on classical Greek and Roman text interpretations, coupled with ignorant and misinformed translations. Academic freedom vanished in the face of ecumenical unease after a college master challenged the wealth and power of the Catholic clergy. With the loss of academic freedom came a concomitant drop in student numbers (Manchester, 1993).

As the Middle Ages gave way to the Renaissance, academic freedom once more became an important tenet of academic life. The reinterpretation of Hellenic and Roman texts led to a redefinition of knowledge through an emphasis on humanism, where religion was an important part of knowledge, but wasn't the sole lens through which all things academic were focused; student numbers began to rise, and new universities sprang up (Manchester, 1993).

Often, professional organizations (e.g., the AAUP) and scholars differentiate between two kinds of academic freedom: individual and institutional. Essentially, individual academic freedom is the freedom of the individual professor/teacher to teach in a manner (content and delivery) they deem best without interference from the academy, school board, or the government. Institutional academic freedom allows the university administration (board of trustees) or local school board to pursue its end without interference from the government (Standler, 1999, p. 4). Institutional academic freedom is the freedom of the academy to determine for itself on academic grounds: (1) who may teach, (2) what may be taught, (3) how it shall be taught, and (4) who may be admitted to study [paraphrased from concurring opinion in *Sweezy v. New Hampshire*, 354 U.S. 234, 263 (1957)].

The relationship between individual and institutional academic freedom is interesting—sometimes they're symbiotic, sometimes they're in conflict with each other. The two academic freedoms are mutually dependent because, "[i]n a very real sense...the *institutional* [academic freedom] recognized in many judicial opinions may be viewed as the sum of acts of *individual* faculty academic freedom. Conflict between these two notions may thus become illusory (Euben, 2002, p. 6)." Quite often, however, individual and institutional academic freedoms are in conflict and, furthermore, it is institutional academic freedom that usually "trumps" individual academic freedom. Katheryn Katz, in "The First Amendment's Protection of Expressive Activity in the University Classroom: A Constitutional Myth," writes,

> The question of which institution [i.e., legislative, judiciary, or executive] has the authority to scrutinize, criticize, and "penalize" the written or oral expression of faculty members on academic subjects has one answer: that authority lies solely within the educational institution, not

the legislature, judiciary, or even executive branches of government... Evidently, the judiciary has not and will not side with the individual faculty members in disputes of this nature. If the issue is the protection to be accorded a truly provocative classroom utterance, there is little reason to expect the faculty member to prevail. And there is even less reason to believe the judiciary will review scholarly writing for evidence of First Amendment violations. In sum, if speech or writing are on "academic subjects," their [i.e., the professors'/teachers'] contents are subject to institutional review, free of judicial oversight. If classroom utterances are on nonacademic or unassigned subjects, they can be penalized because the professor [teacher] is not doing her or his assigned task (Katz, 1983).

Is the individual academic freedom of the high school teacher as protected as that of the university professor? The answer is a resounding "**NO.**" Professor Katz notes, "[the] higher the level of education involved, the more reluctant the judiciary is to interfere with administrative discretion in academic matters (Katz, 1983, p. 932). Ronald B. Standler opines, "academic freedom *does not apply* [author's emphasis] to teachers in elementary and high schools." Some of the reasons enumerated in support of this opinion are:

▼ School teachers teach well-known facts and methods to their pupils. University professors often teach cutting-edge knowledge to advanced students, and can be actively involved in the creation of new knowledge.

▼ University professors are routinely expected to write scholarly works for peer-reviewed publications; school teachers rarely do this.

▼ School teachers usually have only a bachelor's or master's degree with a major subject in "education," whereas university professors have [often] earned a doctoral degree in the subject they teach.

▼ School teachers use textbooks that are chosen by state educational committees [or, at least, with some local school board oversight]; university professors make their own selection of textbooks. [In fairness, it should be noted that university professors are often subject to departmental decisions, policies, and guidelines.]

▼ School teachers have pupils between the ages of 5 and 18, while university professors have students who are at least 18 years of age. Traditionally, public policy offers much more protection and regulation for the education of children than for the education of adults.

▼ Though somewhat oversimplified: The job of school teachers is to impart a specified / recognized body of knowledge to their students; the job of university professors is to teach students how to think and reason critically (Standler, 1999, p. 12).

According to John Strope Jr., in *In our minds, the legal myth dies slowly!* (National Association of Secondary School Principals Bulletin, 1999), earlier in the 20th century courts were more willing to protect the fundamental right of academic freedom at the public school level. Lately, courts have been increasingly unwilling to rule in favor of the teacher, and increasingly "...willing to rely on the judgment of the decision makers, i.e., administrators and school boards." Strope illustrates this with the following: before 1980, teachers won against school boards approximately 50 percent of the time; in the 1990s, teachers won 19 percent of the cases targeting academic freedom. He sees this as evidence that academic freedom is under assault. "The reality is that academic freedom for K-12 public school teachers, as most conceived its meaning, is not what it was. If it was not a myth, then it certainly is diminished in its application as a legal doctrine in public schools today (Strope, 1999)."

SOME RELEVANT COURT DECISIONS ON ACADEMIC FREEDOM

Pickering v. Board of Education, 391 U.S. 563 (1968)

This case concerned *extramural utterance*. Pickering was a teacher in an Illinois high school. He wrote a letter to a local newspaper criticizing how the Board of Education had spent tax money on athletic facilities instead of education. He was also critical of how the school's administration was handling a current proposal to increase the tax rate to support public schools. When Pickering's letter was printed, the Board of Education fired him. State courts upheld the Board's action, but the U.S. Supreme Court found that Pickering's right to freedom was violated, and reversed the Illinois Supreme Court (Standler, 2000 and Katz, 1983).

An often cited concept from Pickering is the phrase "a matter of legitimate public concern." Below is the quote that contains this important concept:

More importantly, the question whether a school system requires additional funds is a matter of legitimate public concern on which the judgment of the school administration, including the School Board, cannot, in a society that leaves such question to popular vote, be taken as conclusive. On such a question free and open debate is vital to informed decision-making by the electorate. Teachers are, as a class, the members of a community most likely to have informed and definite opinions as to how funds allotted to the operations of the schools should be spent. Accordingly, it is essential that they be able to speak out freely on such questions without fear of retaliatory dismissal (Pickering, 391 U.S. at 571-2)... [And the final paragraph says,]... [i]n sum, we hold that, in a case such as this, absent proof of false statements knowingly or recklessly made by him, a teacher's exercise of his right to speak on issues of public importance may not furnish the basis for his dismissal from public employment (*Pickering,* 391 U.S. at 574-575).

The reality of Pickering is not as sanguine as one might expect. In fact, "Pickering's letter was greeted by everyone but its main target, the Board, with massive apathy and total disbelief" [391 U.S. at 570]. So, in the end, Pickering got himself fired, yet lent his name to a landmark Supreme Court decision concerning freedom of speech. Other Supreme Court cases [Pickering's so-called progeny, e.g., *Perry v. Sindermann,* 408 U.S. 593 (1972) and *Mt. Healthy City Board of Education v. Doyle,* 429 U.S. 274 (1977)] have been decided similarly to *Pickering*—that is, public employees may not have their employment terminated as a result of extramural free speech (Standler, 2000).

Hetrick v. Martin, 480 F.2d 705, 709 (6th Cir. 1973), cert. den., 414 U.S. 1075 (1973).

This case is an example in which institutional academic freedom was in conflict with individual academic freedom. Dr. Phyllis Hetrick, a non-tenured assistant professor of English at Eastern Kentucky University (EKU), had her contract terminated because her teaching philosophy, or "pedagogical attitude," was too progressive and didn't conform with the views of the (tenured) department faculty, or with the EKU administration. The Court of Appeals noted:

The school administration considered the students as generally unsophisticated and as having "somewhat restrictive backgrounds," and for this reason apparently expected the teachers to teach on a basic level, to stress fundamentals and to follow conventional teaching patterns, in a word, to "go by the book." Plaintiff's evidence, on the other hand, tended to show that her teaching emphasized student responsibility and freedom to organize class time and out-of-class assignments in terms of student interest, all in an effort, she claimed, to teach them how to think rather than merely to accept and to parrot what they had heard.

According to Standler, EKU didn't show that Hetrick was an ineffective teacher or an incompetent scholar; Hetrick was fired because her teaching style irritated the administration. In a sarcastic admonition, Standler opines, "Instead of seeing Dr. Hetrick as the problem, the real problem is that the EKU administration was admitting students who could not do college-level work, then dumbing down the academic program to accommodate those substandard students....[Later, he concludes,]...[f]or someone who believes that university administrators are intelligent and enlightened people, who not only tolerate but also respect individual differences of style and mannerisms, the behavior of EKU was appalling" (Standler, 1999, p. 11).

Sweezy v. New Hampshire, 354 U. S. 234 (1957).

The opinions voiced in *Sweezy* are quite eloquent and noble. Although *Sweezy* is often cited as a landmark decision involving academic freedom, the case was actually decided with respect to the Due Process Clause of the Fourteenth Amendment. Sweezy was a self-described "classical Marxist" and a "socialist." He gave a guest lecture at the University of New Hampshire and co-authored an article that deplored the use of violence by the United States and other capitalist countries. In 1954, the U.S. was still in the throes of McCarthyism. The Attorney General of New Hampshire summoned and interrogated Sweezy about his affiliation with, and knowledge of, the N.H. Progressive Party. Sweezy denied being a member of the Communist Party or being a part of any program that sought to overthrow the government by means of force or violence. Thereafter, Sweezy refused to answer other questions like:

"Was she, Nancy Sweezy, your wife, active in the formation of the Progressive Citizens of America?"

"Didn't you tell the class at the University of New Hampshire on Monday, March 22, 1954, that Socialism was inevitable in this country?"

"Did you in this last lecture on March 22, or in any of the former lectures espouse the theory of dialectical materialism?" (Sweezy, 354 U.S. at 244).

A Superior Court judged Sweezy to be in contempt because he wouldn't answer certain questions. The N.H. Supreme Court affirmed. Sweezy appealed to the U.S. Supreme Court. The Court held that the appellant's rights and the Due Process Clause of the 14th Amendment were violated, and reversed the N. H. Supreme Court judgment.

As mentioned earlier, some important statements emerged from Sweezy. Below are two such quotes often mentioned with respect to academic freedom:

Merely to summon a witness and compel him, against his will, to disclose the nature of his past expressions and associations is a measure of governmental interference in these matters. These are rights which are safeguarded by the Fourteenth Amendment. We believe that there was an unquestionable invasion of the petitioner's liberties in the areas of academic freedom and political expression—areas in which government should be extremely reticent to tread. The essentiality of freedom in the community of American universities is almost self-evident. No one should underestimate the vital role in a democracy that is played by those who guide and train our youth. To impose any strait jacket upon the intellectual leaders in our colleges and universities would imperil the future of our Nation. No field of education is so thoroughly comprehended by man that new discoveries cannot yet be made. Particularly is that true in the social sciences, where few, if any, principles are accepted as absolutes. Scholarship cannot flourish in an atmosphere of suspicion and distrust. Teachers and students must always remain free to inquire, to study and to evaluate, to gain new maturity and understanding; otherwise our civilization will stagnate and die (Sweezy, 354 U.S. at 250).

After reading these moving words from Chief Justice Warren, one might think that the Supreme Court will go to great lengths to support (individual) academic freedom in schools and universities. The reality is that Sweezy was *not* a professor, just a guest lecturer; and since Sweezy was not an academician, "this case is *not* about academic freedom, and any remarks about academic freedom are, at best, only obiter dicta (Standler, 1999, p. 6).

Although the Supreme Court has recognized academic freedom as a First Amendment right, academic freedom is not an explicit right guaranteed by the Constitution. "Academic freedom is a concept that is neither precisely defined nor convincingly justified from legal principles" (Standler, 1999, p.1); as a result, the scope of the right of academic freedom for professors [teachers] remains unclear (Euben, 2002, p.1). An analysis of judicial decisions indicates that (1) individual academic freedom is more likely to be affirmed in cases involving university professors than in situations involving K-12 teachers; and (2) when institutional academic freedom is in conflict with individual academic freedom, the judicial system is reluctant to interfere with the judgment of the university administration or the local school board and, thus, these cases are usually decided in favor of the institution. Be creative, but follow the rules and guidelines of your local school district policy.

TEACHER EVALUATION

In the State of Washington, the Superintendent of Public Instruction establishes and may amend the minimum criteria for the evaluation of the professional performance capabilities and development of certificated classroom teachers and certificated support personnel. For classroom teachers the criteria is developed in the following categories:

1. Instructional Skill—Competency in designing and conducting lesson plans.

2. Classroom Management—Competency in organizing the physical/human elements in the educational setting.

3. Professional Preparation and Scholarship—Demonstrate knowledge, principles, and commitment to the profession.

4. Effort Toward Improvement When Needed—Demonstrate awareness of strengths for professional growth.

5. Handling of Student Discipline and Attendance Problems—Ability to manage human dynamics occurring at school.

6. Interest in Teaching Pupils—Demonstrate commitment, enthusiasm, and enjoyment in working with students.

7. Knowledge of Subject Matter—Demonstrate depth of knowledge of content areas (Common School Manual, 2003).

Chapter

5

SEARCH AND SEIZURE

The Fourteenth Amendment to the U.S. Constitution prohibits any state from depriving "any person of life, liberty, or property without due process of law." In this context, "state" includes political subdivisions of states, such as cities, counties, and school districts.

Which rights are protected? The Fourteenth Amendment has been interpreted by the U.S. Supreme Court to mean that at least some of the same freedoms guaranteed against Federal intrusion by the Bill of Rights were later guaranteed against state intrusion of those rights which are necessary to our "scheme of ordered liberty" and are said to be "incorporated" into the Fourteenth Amendment and "applied to the states." Thus, even though the Bill of Rights as originally written served to restrict only the federal government, much of it has now been applied to the states and serves to limit both state and federal governmental actions. Action by the public school is considered to be action by the government. Both the Fourth and the First Amendments have been applied to the states via the Fourteenth Amendment.

All state and local officials, including school officials, are bound by the state's Constitution; however, there is no prohibition on states providing greater protection of individual liberty than the federal Constitution requires. In cases involving school searches, Washington courts have treated both the Washington Constitution and the federal Constitution as setting the same standard.

Despite several recent tragedies, schools continue to be among the safest places in America. Even so, each day serious offenses that involve violence, weapons, and drugs are committed by and against school children. These offenses endanger the welfare of children and teachers and disrupt the educational process. The situation demands a decisive response.

One of the best ways to keep weapons, drugs, tobacco, alcohol, and other forms of contraband out of our schools and away from children is to make it clear that school officials will keep a watchful eye and will intervene decisively at the first sign of trouble. It is essential for school officials to be diligent and to pursue all lawful means to keep guns and other weapons, drugs, and alcohol off the school grounds.

The need to keep order and to maintain a safe, well-disciplined school environment must be balanced against the rights of students to be free from unreasonable searches and seizures. The challenge is to achieve a delicate and appropriate balance between the need to protect the rights of students and teachers to be safe and the need to respect the rights guaranteed to all citizens under the Fourth Amendment. While the Fourth Amendment imposes significant limitations on the authority of police and school officials to conduct searches and to seize property, the law provides enough flexibility for school officials to protect students from harm and to enforce school codes of conduct. Indeed, in *New Jersey v. T.L.O.*, United States Supreme Court decision expressly recognizes the authority of school officials to conduct reasonable searches of students and their property. The Court's ruling provides school officials with an important tool with which to address the security problems posed by students who use, possess, or distribute drugs, alcohol, or weapons.

As future educators, it is important for you to know and define "search". A "search" entails conduct by government officials (including public school employees) that involves intrusion into a person's protected privacy interests, for example, the examination of items or places that are not in the open and exposed to public view. This is usually accomplished by "peeking", "poking", or "prying" into a place or item shielded from public view in a closed container, such as a locker, desk, purse, backpack, briefcase, folder, or article of clothing.

The term "seizure" needs to be defined as well. "Seizure" is used to describe two distinct types of governmental action. A seizure occurs when a government official interferes with an individual's freedom of movement (the seizure of person) or when a government official interferes with an individual's possessory interests in property (the seizure of an object).

The Fourth Amendment played a key role in setting forth the general rules on search and seizure. The Fourth Amendment states:

> The right of the people to be secure in their persons, houses, papers and effects against unreasonable searches and seizures shall not be violated, and no warrants shall issue, but upon probable cause, supported by oath or affirmation, and particularly describing the place to be searched and the persons or things to be seized.

According to Tom McBride of the Washington Association of Prosecuting Attorneys, search is anything that involves intrusion into a student's protected privacy interests, usually by examining items or places that are not open to the public view.

Search is a very controversial issue in the public school system today. Many schools and parents have questions and disagreements as to where the line needs to be drawn in order to protect the rights of students. There are many court cases pending as to what exactly is constitutional when it comes to schools and searches. Many of the reasons brought forth defending the right to search students stems from protection and prevention actions in order to put a stop to the violence that plagues school systems today. However, there are also many searches conducted in which no valid reasons are given as to why certain students are subject to these personal violations and other students are not.

There are many different types of searches conducted today. Examples include searching backpacks or purses, opening a book, patting down a jacket, passing through a metal detector, or ordering a student to empty their pockets. There are also more intrusive searches such as looking through lockers, or vehicles, or even conducting strip searches. These searches cannot all be conducted by just anyone and usually need strong evidence presented for their validity.

School officials need only "reasonable suspicion" before they may conduct a search. However, it is important to take into account the seriousness of the problem in order to justify a search of any kind. Important factors to take into account include the student's age, history, and school record, the prevalence and seriousness of the problem, the need to search immediately, and the reliability of the information used in order to justify the search (McBride, 2001). When a school official is conducting a search there must be reasonable suspicion to begin the search, and it must remain reasonable for the scope, duration, and intensity. Common sense and proper motive should always be seriously considered when it comes to searching students and their belongings. The problem underlying this controversial issue is that many disagree as to the definition and classification of what determines "reasonable suspicion".

Because the Supreme Court has determined that schools have a substantial interest in maintaining order within school districts, a more flexible standard of search procedures are available for school officials, as opposed to law enforcement officers. School officials, unlike the police, do not need to obtain a warrant or determine probable cause before conducting a search. School officials need only "reasonable suspicion" that the search will produce evidence that the student broke laws or school rules. However, to be permissible, the method of search must not be excessively intrusive in regard to age, gender, and nature of the suspected infraction. Reasonable suspicion is defined as observation of a specific and describable behavior leading one reasonably to believe that a particular student is engaging in or has engaged in prohibited conduct. Searches based upon reasonable suspicion must be initiated and conducted by school officials. Searches using or in conjunction with law enforcement officers are held to a more stringent standard and validation process (Action Guide, 1996).

The U.S. Supreme Court has not decided whether students have legitimate expectations of privacy in school property, such as lockers and desks. School lockers issued to individual students for the storage of personal belongings and school supplies may be considered private space. Thus, students may have an increased expectation of privacy for the locker's contents. Students have less expectation of privacy for classroom desks and their contents. These desks are unsecured and available for use by all students throughout the school day. Courts are more likely to uphold searches of school property when students have reduced expectations of privacy. At the beginning of each school year, officials might inform the student body that random searches of desks and lockers may be conducted at any time. They must consider these spaces public and not private. Furthermore, school property inspections may then be implemented on a regular basis to further reduce students' expectations of privacy. Otherwise, the practice of not searching might negate the search policy by raising the expectation of privacy in such areas.

Vehicles parked on school grounds are also available for search. Parking lots are considered school property and are subject to search whenever reasonable suspicion occurs. Before conducting vehicle searches, students need to be warned of the upcoming searches and reasons for the searches taking place. Under limited circumstances, unsuspicious, random vehicle searches may be conducted to procure weapons and/or drugs. Schools will need to demonstrate that they have a very serious drug and/or weapons problem in order to justify such a search policy. Once again, school officials must adequately inform students that their vehicles are subject to random search while parked on school property. Vehicle searches must be conducted uniformly or by systematic random selection. Allowing school officials to decide which vehicles will be searched allows for undue discretion and the opportunity for discrimination. Students may also consent to any type of search, thus making it legal and reasonable. However, student consent must be voluntary and knowingly given (McBride, 2001).

There are also several alternative search techniques available to school officials. The use of trained narcotics dogs to sniff objects rather than to sniff people is not considered a search within the boundaries of the Fourth Amendment; therefore, these types of searches may be conducted at any time and with no level of suspicion. Narcotics dogs may sniff any locker, desk, student vehicle on a school lot, or any item of personal property that has been discarded or abandoned. After the dog has alerted officials to a particular locker, vehicle, or other such item, reasonable suspicion has been established and school officials may progress into a more thorough search. Most courts agree that using a sniff dog on individual students does constitute a search and must therefore be based upon prior reasonable suspicion (McBride, 2001).

The use of metal detectors in schools has generally been upheld in the court systems. As with their use in airports and courts, metal detector use in schools is deemed minimally intrusive. Prior to implementing metal detector use, schools should be able to demonstrate that there is a serious problem, which the detectors could help to reduce. Schools must also avoid selecting on whom the detectors will be used. It must be used on every student or in a systematically random manner, such as every third student. However, metal detector use is only justifiable in searching for weapons. Other contraband discovered by use of the detector may only be seized.

There are many factors to take into account when conducting a search on a student. School officials and law enforcement officials both need to take extreme caution when searching students. Searches need to be based upon valid evidence in order to be held up in the court systems (Action Guide, 1996).

When conducting a search on a student, a teacher or school official must make appropriate choices. Some things to always practice in order to make your searches safe and valid are to make sure another teacher or student is present during any type of search. Be sure to document any search administered and record any findings. When determining whether or not there are reasonable grounds for a search always take into account all circumstances, including age, history, and school records along with the seriousness of the problem. In making sure your search is valid, use common sense. If you are looking for a gun, it is not necessary to search the littlest coin pouch in a purse or backpack. Another piece of advice is to stop the search once the object is found.

When possible, searching should always be performed in a location away from the general populace in order to maintain a student's privacy and decrease the level of intrusiveness. Do not use students to search or seize evidence; this is a procedure that should be strictly administered by only school officials or law enforcement officers. Last, use common sense and be on the side of the student before you jump to accusations of sus-pected violations in policy. Allow for the students to come forward on their own with any evidence to decrease the necessity of any kind of search as well as keeping the relationships less violated and intrusive (Action Guide, 1996).

Government officials must have a warrant issued by a judge to arrest or search. There are a few narrowly drawn exceptions to the warrant re-quirement. One such exception applies to searches of students conducted by school authorities. There is no need for a school official to obtain a search warrant before searching a student's person or locker, provided there is a legitimate ground justifying the search. In *New Jersey v. T.L.O.* 469 U.S. 325 (1985), a female student's purse was searched by an assistant principal who found her in a smoke-filled bathroom and asked her to empty her purse on the table. She complied, and not only was tobacco found, but also drug paraphernalia and other suspicious items, which led the assistant principal to suspect drug dealing. The student was suspended and she sued the school authorities on the basis of an unreasonable search. The Court held that a warrantless search of a student's purse for ciga-rettes, after she was found smoking in the bathroom, was justified be-cause the school authorities had reasonable grounds to believe the purse contained cigarettes in violation of school regulations.

School officials may only search students within reasonable limits. Generally, a more intrusive search will require greater justification and validation in order to be upheld by the courts. Searching a student's jacket or pockets would require less suspicion than a physical pat down or strip-search. Strip-searches are highly intrusive and should only be conducted when based upon probable cause.

In *State ex rel. Galford v. Anthony*, 433 S.E.2d 41 (1993), the principal strip-searched a student suspected of theft.

A teacher at Marlinton Middle School discovered $100 was missing from her purse that she left in her empty classroom. The principal suspected Mark, a 14 year old, who had been assigned to help the janitor. The principal questioned Mark, who admitted he had been in the classroom to empty the trash can but denied taking the money. The principal asked Mark to pull out his pockets and roll down his socks. Discovering nothing, the principal took Mark into the boys' bathroom and had him pull down his pants and pull open the front, and then the back, of his underwear. The money had been tucked into the back of Mark's underwear. Criminal proceedings were brought against Mark, who argued the search of his underwear was unreasonable and therefore the evidence discovered through the search could not be used against him. The trial court rejected this argument. Mark appealed and the decision was reversed. Unless it is suspected that a student poses a danger to others, for example, if he is carrying a weapon, a strip search by school officials is presumed to be excessively intrusive. If school officials have reasonable grounds to believe a student is hiding some evidence of wrong doing, they may make a limited search without first obtaining a warrant. This standard is substantially less rigorous than the standard applied to police dealing with adult suspects.

Although the principal had reasonable grounds to conduct a less intrusive search of Mark and his belongings, the scope of search performed in the bathroom was unreasonable and was not justified (*New Jersey v. T.L.O*).

A strip-search is considered extremely intrusive and would not be a reasonable method in most circumstances. In *State v. Sweeney*, 56 Wn. App. 42 (1989), the court of appeals threw out drug evidence obtained in the strip-search of a student in a school-like setting. The court stated that searching the student's pockets was acceptable but searching inside his underwear was not. Note that it should not be necessary to undress a student to determine whether he or she is carrying a weapon.

Under police power, a warrant is required before a search takes place. Probable cause exists when the police provide evidence sufficient to presume that a subject may be involved in criminal activities. In contrast to police power, school officials may search a student based on nothing more than a *reasonable suspicion* that the student has drugs. This is an easier standard to meet than the police's probable cause requirement.

GUIDELINE FOR SEARCH

To determine whether a search is appropriate, the school officials should consider the following factors:

1. The child's age, history, and school record.

2. The prevalence and seriousness of the problem.

3. The exigency to make the search without delay.

4. The probative value of and reliability of the information used as justification for the search.

In *Keuhn v. Renton School District*, 103 Wn.2d 594 (1985), the Washington Supreme Court held that a search was not necessary when school authorities organized parents to carry out a pre-announced search for alcohol in students' luggage as a condition of each student's participation in a field trip to Canada. Since school authorities had no reasonable basis to believe any particular student possessed alcohol, the court concluded the search unlawful.

A search is allowed if under all the circumstances it is reasonable. The search must be justified before it begins, and its scope must be reasonably related to the circumstances which justified it. This means the method of searching must be reasonable, and the places searched must also be reasonable (*State v. Sweeney*, 56 Wn. App. 820 (1990)). Searching all students before a school field trip, "just to avoid the possibility of trouble," is not permitted.

To meet the reasonable belief standard, it would have been necessary for officials to have some basis for believing that drugs or alcohol would be found in the luggage of each individual student searched. In any sufficiently large group there is a statistical probability that someone will possess contraband. The Fourth Amendment demands more than a generalized probability; it requires that the suspicion be particularized with respect to each individual searched.

CASE STUDIES ON SEARCH

Class Action Suit

During a metal detection search, high school students claimed that school officials touched them inappropriately. The touching, according to the students, was sexual. The touching occurred even when the metal detector did not detect anything suspicious. Students tried to file a class action lawsuit against the school.

1. Was the search reasonable?

2. Were the students justified in taking action to file a lawsuit?

3. Do you foresee any sexual harassment claim in this scenario?

Car Search

Ms. Johnson consented to a search of her car that had been stopped by an officer for a traffic violation and evidence was discovered that was used to convict the respondent of unlawfully possessing drugs. In a habeas corpus proceeding, the District Court found her guilty of possession. Ms. Johnson appealed and the Appeals Court reversed the decision.

1. On what technical grounds was Ms. Johnson basing her appeal?

2. When the subject of a search is not in custody, do the Fourth and Fourteenth Amendments require that the subject demonstrates that the consent was in fact, voluntary?

Chapter

CHILD ABUSE

Introduction

The most dangerous period for the child is from two months of age to three years. The abused, battered child is most vulnerable during these years when he or she is most defenseless and least capable of meaningful social interaction. Some researchers have stated that the first six months are the most dangerous for the child. Others like Bennie and Sclare have reported that, in their sample, battered children were usually from two to four months old. It is entirely possible that these data are somewhat skewed, since the vulnerability of a child to physical damage is greater at a younger age. At the same time, older children may also be subject to physical abuse, but they might not appear in case studies because their age and physical durability make them less vulnerable to serious physical damage caused by abuse. However, as future state employees, we must be able to pay attention to the negative social factors that may affect our students.

Areen states, "As far as developing new strategies of intervention, it is now necessary to stop thinking of child abuse as having a single cause: the mental aberrations of the parents." Studies have shown that physical abuse of children is not a uniform phenomenon with one set of causal factors, but a multi-dimensional phenomenon. Therefore, it is time to start thinking about the multiple social factors that influence child abuse. For example, "if unemployment and social class are important contextual variables, then strategies to prevent child abuse should aim at alleviating the disastrous effect of being poor in an affluent society" (Areen, 1992).

CHILD ABUSE AND NEGLECT

The United States government has the right to exercise police power, and the government is entrusted with the responsibility of looking after the health, safety, and welfare of all citizens. In the common law doctrine of *parens patriea*, the state acts as a guardian over all its people. This guardianship extends to care for children who have been either abused or neglected by their parents. Statistics show that high numbers of children are abused. As a result, all 50 states have statutes dealing with child abuse and neglect. The statute protects children under the age of eighteen, but the scope of protection and definitions of abuse vary among states. The severity of the problem, however, is highlighted by nationwide mandatory reporting of suspected abuse and neglect.

Undoubtedly, as teachers you will have suspicions that a child is suffering from abuse. How to deal with the situation is a dilemma for many. To know what to do, you must be aware of what child abuse is and what it constitutes. Many teachers do not feel they have been trained well enough to really know this.

Concerning the decision making process used by teachers in cases of suspected child abuse, research have found that although teachers work with children for a large part of the day, many do not know how to handle child abuse. Other researchers have similar findings. Many teachers do not report abuse because they do not know exactly what it is and what are its signs, nor do they know how to report it. Although teachers have an increased awareness of what child abuse is, the training and education they need to confront the problem has not grown in proportion to their awareness.

Abuse
1) neglect
2) physical & emotional
DEFINITION OF CHILD ABUSE
3) sexual

Child abuse is traditionally divided into three areas: neglect, physical and emotional abuse, and sexual abuse. According to U.S. Public Law 92-247, child abuse is the physical and mental injury, sexual, and negligent treatment of a child under the age of 18 by a person who is responsible for the child's welfare, under circumstances which indicate that the child's health and welfare is harmed or threatened. Neglect, on the other hand generally refers to the disregard of the physical, emotional, and moral needs of children or adolescents. This includes children who are dirty, malnourished, unattended, overworked, and those who do not attend school regularly.

Physical and emotional abuse refers to intentional behavior directed toward a child by parent(s) or caregivers to cause pain, injury, or death. The most common forms of physical abuse include slapping, spanking, hitting with objects, grabbing, and shoving. The most common forms of emotional abuse include steady putdowns, humiliation, labeling, name-calling, lying, ignoring, or anything else that indicates a lack of expressed love and affection.

Sexual abuse, or incest, is abuse that is perpetrated on a child by a member of that child's family group and includes not only sexual intercourse but also any act designed to stimulate a child sexually or to use that child for sexual stimulation. The most common sexual abuse cases take place between the father and daughter; however, there are studies that show that sexual abuse may be more prevalent among brothers and sisters.

ABUSE OF CHILDREN BY PARENTS

There are many reasons parents abuse children. Sometimes the parent may set out to discipline rather than abuse a child. The parent, in a fit of rage, might accidentally grab the child by its arm, breaking it. The parent did not set out to abuse the child but none-the-less the child has been abused. Another example of unintentional abuse is when busy parents neglect a child. Each parent assumes the other is feeding and bathing the child, but neither is doing these things. Thus, the child is being neglected and the parents could be accused of abuse.

Another reason parents may abuse their child is because they have negative views of the child. The parent, in this case, may not physically abuse the child but emotionally abuse him or her, telling the child she or he is worthless and will never amount to anything, or constantly yelling. The child will not have any physical signs of abuse, but will be scarred emotionally.

Lack of family and peer support is another reason for child abuse. Parents can feel stressed without the support that all parents need to successfully raise a child. Abuse in this case can manifest itself in any form.

Abuse can occur at any point in a child's life. If a parent is suffering from higher than normal levels of life stress and personal distress, that parent can become abusive. In this case, the abuse could come and go, putting additional stress on the child because of the uncertainty of what will happen next. One day the parent could be really affectionate, and the next, yelling and hitting the child.

If a parent has poor problem-solving skills in child-related situations, this can also lead to abuse. It is easy to become frustrated with a child if the child is not doing as he or she is told. A parent with good coping skills can easily deal with this, but a parent with poor coping skills will become angry and be more likely to strike out, either verbally or physically. Parents who verbally and physically assault their children may have harsh disciplinary strategies. They may have been raised in the same way and know no other way to discipline their children.

Forty five percent of physically abusive adults meet the criteria for alcohol or drug disorders during their lifetimes. The rate of child neglect is even higher than that of physical abuse. This does not mean that because parents abuse drug or alcohol they will abuse their children; it is, however, more likely that abuse will occur.

The last cause of child abuse is when the mother was herself a victim of incest. A child of an incest-surviving mother is at a higher risk for sexual abuse than a child whose mother was not a victim of incest. Many different incidences contribute to child abuse by parents, and just a few examples have been discussed.

ABUSE OF CHILDREN BY TEACHERS

When a teacher abuses a child, it is usually sexual abuse. This is not to say that a teacher cannot abuse children in other ways. The number of male and female teachers that abuse their students is unequal. Teachers who sexually abuse children in their care range from kindergarten through high school teachers and administrators.

During the 2001-2004 school year, authorities convicted a few educators in Washington State of sexually abusing children, and many more have been accused since then. Of the educators who have been convicted of having some sort of inappropriate contact with their students, one was a special education teacher and one was a kindergarten teacher. Of those who have been accused but not yet convicted, one is a school principal and one is a technology instructor.

You may now be asking yourself: "Why so many cases surfacing?" the answer to this is simple, according to school attorneys and investigative authorities. It is not that more educators are abusing the children in their care. The fact is people are more willing to report sex offenders so that more perpetrators are being caught. More cases are also being reported because school administrators are beginning to be more aggressive when following up on reports that an educator is sexually abusing a child. This is due to court cases that show that administrators can be held liable if it goes unreported when the administrator knew of the problem.

To prevent sexual abuse of students in the schools, there needs to be background checks for every school employee. This will not eliminate all abuse by educators, but it will help to reduce the number of people who re-offend. This will not work in all cases because some school districts hide the fact that there were allegations of sexual abuse when an employee has resigned. Yet, it will eliminate those who have been charged and/or convicted of abusing a student from obtaining a job in another school district.

Child Abuse Facts

There are many statistics for child abuse. It is a fact, in my opinion, that many people do not want to acknowledge that abuse of children is happening every day in every city at all economical levels. It is not only poor children who are being abused.

In 2001, there were one million children who were reported as abused or neglected in the United States. In the same year, there were another two million reported yet unconfirmed cases of child abuse. Of those children, it is estimated that 47 percent suffered from neglect, 30 percent from physical abuse, and 11 percent from sexual abuse.

In 2001 alone, 2,000 child deaths were caused by abuse or neglect. It is estimated that 10,000 more child deaths were unreported because of misdiagnoses, and incomplete or flawed investigations and autopsies. Of the 2,000 known child deaths caused by abuse, 90 percent of the children were under the age of four (Personal conversation with a CPS work, 2003).

Indicators of Abused Children

There are physical and behavioral signs expressed by children that may indicate that some form of abuse is taking place. Any of these indicators should be taken seriously and appropriate action should be taken immediately.

For neglect, the physical signs include a child who is underweight or small for his or her age, is always hungry, is not kept clean, is inappropriately dressed for weather, or has not received needed medical/dental care. The behavioral signs include a child who begs or steals food, frequently arrives at child-care early and leaves later than expected, has frequent, unexplained absences, or is overtired or listless.

For physical and emotional abuse, the physical signs include unexplained bruises or welts in unusual places, or several bruises or welts in different stages of healing. Signs can also show up as unusual shapes or clusters, unexplained burns, unexplained broken bones or dislocations, unexplained bites, or explanations for injuries that differ from that of the parent or caretaker. Behavioral signs include the child telling you she has been hurt by parents or others, the child becoming frightened when other children cry, the child saying the parents or care-takers deserve to be punished, or the child being afraid of certain people.

For sexual abuse, the physical signs include difficulty walking or sitting, wearing torn, stained or bloody underwear, pain, swelling, or itching of genitals, bruises, cuts, or bleeding on genitals or the anal area, pain when urinating or defecating, a discharge from the vagina or penis, or a sexually-transmitted disease. The behavioral signs include acting withdrawn, being over-involved in fantasy, acting much older than the actual age, displaying sophisticated or bizarre sexual knowledge or behavior, exhibiting excessive or unusual touching of genitals, or trying to hurt oneself.

THE ROLE OF THE SCHOOL

Schools represent an important system involved in safeguarding the well-being of children. They often are the first intervening system to interact with the victimized child, to assess an incident, report suspected abuse, and provide supportive services for the child. Educators in this process may play an integral role; however, teachers often lack confidence in their range of knowledge of sexual abuse and their abilities to provide appropriate intervention. Consequently, as society struggles to address the rising tide of incidents of child sexual abuse, educators often find themselves inadequately prepared to confront the growing number of victims in the classroom.

All 50 states have reporting laws that identify schoolteachers and administrators as mandated reporters of child abuse to child protective service agencies. Despite this legal responsibility, educators typically remain unclear about applicable laws and reporting procedures. Among professionals who interact with children, teachers are the least knowledgeable about child abuse information, and studies indicate that relatively few education training programs require curriculum on child victimization for certification.

Even when teachers are aware of their mandatory obligations, they are significantly less likely to report sexual abuse than are other education professionals. Many school reporting procedures diffuse responsibility to designated reporters; however, this policy may contribute to teachers' ignoring their duty to report. If educators believe that the responsibility for reporting abuse lies with the administrator, they may expect someone else to act on suspicions of victimization. Although teachers are mandated to respond to suspected incidents of child sexual abuse, the inability to recognize that a problem exists for a child is among the first barriers to utilizing appropriate intervention services that may work toward ensuring the emotional and physical safety of the child. It is a common tendency of people to distort information cognitively to match their view. In an attempt to protect ourselves against the horrors of the reality of abuse, we may cloud ourselves in denial. This denial provides a safe haven for adults who may excuse lack of protective action under the guise of "I didn't know." Educators often feel reassured by the myth that sexual abuse is not a problem among affluent, educated, and religious families. In reality, child sexual abuse occurs among all family types. Regardless of the population demographics of the school setting, educators must assume responsibility for acting on a reasonable level of suspicion for abuse.

When a child feels safe enough to disclose abuse, teachers who intervene may continue to play an important role by supporting the child and creating a classroom environment conducive to the child's emotional well-being. It is important to clearly give children the message that they are not responsible for the abuse. Upon disclosure, educators may feel overwhelmed by their shock, anger, and fear. The way that these reactions are managed may affect the outcome for the child.

Please note that abuse can happen in any family, regardless of income level, education, race, religion, culture, and type of employment or family structure. You do not have to prove that child abuse has occurred in order to report child abuse. You only need *reasonable cause to believe* that a child has suffered abuse or neglect. Reasonable cause to believe is based on a child disclosing abuse to you, direct observation, signs or symptoms exhibited by a child or family, or a combination of these. When you have a feeling that something is wrong in a child's life, start to pay close attention to the child's behaviors and needs.

GROOMING

Grooming is getting a victim ready for abuse, getting a victim closer to the abuser, and establishing a bond and dependency relationship. This abuser is adept at:

▼ Intimidating with body language or loud voice

▼ Using physical force, including grabbing and carrying the victim

▼ Asking the victim's permission (e.g., "I enjoy this. Is it okay?")

▼ Forcing the victim to look at pornographic materials

▼ Forcing the victim to wear or model inappropriate clothing (photographing them)

▼ Desensitizing the victim (e.g., swimming together, wrestling, telling dirty jokes)

▼ Giving privileges, gifts, (e.g., limited discipline)

▼ Peer-like involvement in victim's life

▼ Befriending the victim; becoming the victim's confidant, being the good listener, pretending concern, sharing dreams

▼ Attempting to convince the victim that responsibility for the abuse is shared and that they would both be punished if the abuse were discovered

▼ Frightening the victim: "If you tell, I will go to jail and we'll lose the house. Mom will kill herself. No one will believe you."

▼ Apologizing and promising not to re-offend

▼ Promising to get counseling and bluffing about suicide (Adapted from notes taken in a child abuse session, 2002.)

COMMON SENSE RULES ON TOUCHING

Playing with children in school settings can have an emotionally positive educational aspect. At the same time, touching children has risk. The teacher may be accused of improper touching in some instances. To avoid accusations, she/he has to exercise good judgment in determining whether to touch students and for what purpose. To exercise good judgment regarding touching the educational practitioner must consider the following:

Early elementary: At this age, it is impossible to avoid touching students or avoid the students touching you in the classroom. On the other hand, as the students grow older, teachers may discuss the acceptability of touching and how it should be decreased.

From grades four through nine, male and female children are extremely conscious of their sexuality. According to child psychologists, most accusations of improper touching in schools occur in this age group. Females at this stage are especially sensitive regarding their body development and often view a touch around the chest or back to be sexual in nature. They are also very sensitive about remarks regarding their clothing and physical appearance. School practitioners and other employees of the school district get into trouble with this age group by putting their arms around students' shoulders or around waists. Even the way the educator looks at the student may be suspicious to the child.

Be extremely careful about touching students in this age group. If possible, do not touch these students at all. We usually get into trouble with this group when we attempt to be their confidant or try to counsel troubled children, especially about romantic matters.

Some cultures are very uncomfortable with any form of touching, so teachers need to be sensitive to individual and cultural preferences, and if any students indicate to you by word or action that they are uncomfortable with touching, you should avoid any physical contact. According to counselors, children who have been sexually abused may misperceive a neutral or innocent touch as sexual. Some common trouble areas that need to be avoided are: driving students around in a car; writing cards, notes or letters to students; repeated one-to-one contact with a student, and engaging in social activities with the students (WEA lecture on Child Abuse, 2000).

Chapter

7

TORT LIABILITY

Some who write about education dwell on the dangers of being held responsible for students' injuries. They stress the seriousness of personal liability and the possibilities of disaster for the teacher. According to Johnson and others (1991), this is a seriously distorted impression. It is true that teachers may be held personally liable for injuries that occur because of their negligence, but this is true of every citizen. The notion of tort is derived from the ancient master-servant laws, which means that a master is liable in certain cases for the wrongful acts of his servant. When applied to schools this means that the school district may be charged with liability for the wrongful acts of its teachers and other employees.

Educational practitioners are encouraged to grasp the understanding of tort liability. An offense against the state is a crime and constitutes a positive or negative breach of some duty which an individual owes to the community. A tort is a civil wrong, which causes personal injury or property damage. Torts come from the Latin word *Tortus,* which means twisted. The tort is a wrongful act that causes injury in some way in which the violator is civilly liable, as opposed to a crime in which the violator may be criminally penalized. As stated above, this definition applies to all who live in our society, but the most important aspect of tort that pertains to teachers is the care of children and the full responsibility of their safety.

Hazard, in 1978, stated that every tort action has three elements: (1) a legal duty owed to the plaintiff by the defendant; (2) a breach of that duty, and (3) damages as a proximate result of the breach. The same act may be a crime and a tort. For example, O.J. Simpson was charged with murder (a wrong against the state), a penalty that was going to be imposed through a criminal prosecution. But he was found "not guilty" by a jury. He was later charged with a tort (a civil wrong against the victim) and found guilty. The damages were assessed through civil proceedings. Under tort law a person who causes injury to another is answerable to the injured party for damages: "A person is not liable for every accidental injury. Only if a person intentionally or negligently causes injury will that person be liable."

In some instances teachers can be careless in the supervision of students. Therefore, an understanding of this area of law will help teachers gain increased interest in their responsibility to exercise good judgment in caring for the well-being of students. In assessing the responsibility of the teacher, the Reasonable Man Theory is applied to whether or not a tort has been committed: "Was an action taken that a reasonable person under similar circumstances would, or would not, have taken?" In order for an individual's action to be considered a tort, Peterson and others have established four conditions that must be shown to exist:

1. A duty or obligation that requires one to conform to a certain standard of conduct so as to protect others against unreasonable risk.

2. A failure to act in a manner that conforms to the standard of conduct required.

3. An injury to another caused by failure to act in the manner required.

4. Actual loss or damages to the person or interest of another as a result of the injury.

Peterson and others contend that once a tort has been legally established the person claiming the injury must prove three things: The defendant had a duty to protect the complainant against unreasonable risk or injury; the defendant failed to protect the complainant from injury; and the breach of duty by the defendant was the proximate cause of the complainant's injury. It is obvious that many questions can arise concerning liability out of situations where it is alleged that a student was injured during a period when a teacher failed to supervise. To help teachers understand their responsibility, McCarthy and Cambron cited three major areas of tort action:

1. *Negligence*—the most common tort. It is the failure to comply with an acceptable standard of care: the degree of care expected of a reasonable, prudent person in the same or similar circumstances. The question of negligence frequently arises in schools from a teacher's alleged breach of some duty of care owed to the student.

2. *Intentional torts*—those who are committed with the desire to inflict harm, which includes assault, battery, false imprisonment, trespass, and defamation.

3. *Strict liability*—the injury of a person because of the creation of an unusual hazard.

Although teachers must exercise reasonable care, this does not ensure the safety and well-being of students in their care. Their duty requires only reasonable care: "The teacher's duty of reasonable care includes warning children of any known dangers or risk in school activities." Some activities may require physical conditioning and preparation; the teacher's failure to plan and supervise such physical conditioning may result in liability for negligence. A common broad rule requires teachers to be in their classrooms at all times when students are present. However, the teacher's presence does not necessarily prevent negligence, nor does the teacher's absence always mean negligence. Issues may arise when a teacher must leave a classroom while students are engaged in school activities. The question of negligence is not based on the teacher's absence but on the question of the reasonableness of the teacher's actions. If, under the circumstances, the teacher acted as a reasonably prudent person, the court will not impose tort liability.

Teachers have a unique position in which they are liable for the welfare of children in their care even though it is understood that teachers are *in loco parentis,* which means that the teacher is in place of the parent when the parent is absent. While students are in the care of a teacher, the teacher is responsible for any harm done, whether intentional or not. The teacher is in the position not only to protect the child but also to ensure a safe learning environment for the child. Although rare, intentional torts have occurred against students, and students are then allowed civil compensation for those misdeeds perpetrated against them. Intentional torts also may carry criminal punishment for the accused educator.

The most common form of tort is the "negligent tort" in which the tort occurred as a result of not doing something that a regular person would have done under normal circumstances to prevent injury or even death. Accidents do not fall under this definition of negligent tort. Let us discuss intentional torts.

For a tort to be considered intentional the person committing the tort must know that injury may result from his or her actions. The most common of these intentional torts is assault. Assault is an intentional attempt to cause bodily injury or the fear of bodily injury. In both cases the individual perpetrating the tort is fully aware that the victim may be harmed. However, courts have been somewhat lenient in a few cases since a teacher is also there to discipline students, but only if that discipline is not found to be excessive (Yell, 1999). In the State of Washington, the use of corporal punishment is no longer accepted in the public schools. Teachers are instructed to use the minimal amount of physical contact with students; therefore, intentional torts in Washington may be viewed as malicious. Battery, as opposed to assault, is the result of actual physical harm. Battery is the intentional harm done to a student except in cases of self-defense (Yell, 1999). Intentional torts may not only result in civil liability but also in criminal punishment for the aggressor. This is one of the main differences between intentional tort and negligent tort, and it directly affects the way a court may decide a teacher's liability.

Negligent tort, for educators, is an injury that, although it occurred unintentionally to a student, may have been foreseen by the teacher or administrators. This excludes accidents that occur due to carelessness. Negligent torts fall under many different categories and are not as straight-forward as intentional torts. The first category is the duty to protect. This is a major responsibility of all teachers regardless of students' ages. The duty to protect means that it is the responsibility of the educator to protect children from harm by way of adequate supervision both in the classroom and out of the classroom. Activities that are out of the class-room include field trips, but they may also include rides home by teach-ers. This latter action could even result in accusations of sexual abuse. Teachers allowing students into the school building early in the morning can face a liability, especially if there is minimal supervision in the build-ing (Yell, 1999).

The second category is similar to the first, but it differs in the amount of supervision required for the safety of students. This category is known as reasonable standard of care. The teacher must be aware of the age and activities of the students. For example, a shop teacher would not allow a five year old to work in the shop. The teacher must know the limitations of the students as well as the appropriate precautions for that environ-ment; therefore, an educator must use the appropriate amount of care for those activities. This requires the educator to foresee any possible injuries that may result from a specific activity, which brings up the fourth cat-egory of negligent tort: foresight (Yell, 1999).

Third, the educator must be able to foresee any type of injury that may occur as a result of the activity which that educator is supervising. This also extends to building and equipment safety in the immediate area of the students. The educator must anticipate all injuries, except for accidental injuries, in order to be protected from liability. Science teachers, physical education teachers, special education teachers, and shop teachers are the most at risk for these unforeseen injuries. All of these teachers must be fully aware of all the scenarios that could lead to the injury of a student. Injuries need to be proven as actual injuries to comply with the proof of negligence (Yell, 1999).

The fourth category for negligence is that of actual injury: the injury sustained must be real and not fake. The injury does not always have to be physical, but it must fall under the category of an actual injury in order to prove any sort of negligence. The same goes for intentional torts; the injuries cannot be faked in order to receive civil compensation, or to prove contributory negligence (Yell, 1999).

There are many defenses against liability, but one of the most important is that of "contributory negligence". Contributory negligence is used if it can establish that students did not exercise prudence or caution, contributing to their injuries. Inevitably, children are curious, and if you bring enough attention to a potential problem or hazard in which students may incur some injury, some students may allow curiosity to get the better of them. This can lead to students purposefully putting themselves in danger even when they were warned beforehand. Contributory negligence is very difficult to prove with very young children that have not yet developed a good sense of judgment. Defense against negligence is difficult, but not impossible, and the teaching profession is not the only victim of civil litigation (Yell, 1999).

Liability is a problem in all professions, including construction, trucking, manufacturing, and medicine. Even the law profession is not exempt from the effects of liability. What makes the teaching profession so vulnerable is the fact that children are involved. It plays on the emotions of the parents and the public when an innocent child may have been injured due to negligence. The truth is that the only way to protect teachers from liability is to educate them on what to do when a potential danger to students is discovered and how to remedy the situation as soon as possible. Practice with hypothetical situations is the best way to protect teachers and school districts from liability situations.

Examples of hypothetical situations could include the following: What to do when a potential hazard is present in the building and what steps to take to remedy that situation, or what a teacher should do if students have climbed on top of the school's roof. Should the teacher call administration and inform them? Should the teacher post a sign where the students are playing, which reads "No unauthorized personnel on the roof," or should the teacher ignore the problem and continue with the day as normal? There is no right answer, but no matter what teachers do, they cannot ignore the situation. Ignorance is not a defense. No matter what teachers do to remedy the situation, they must document all of the activities that they do in order to protect themselves from liability, even if the administration does nothing to remedy the situation.

What would teachers do if a student threatened another student in a teacher's presence? It may seem like an empty threat, but a teacher does not know that. Courts could find teachers liable because they are there to protect all students from harm. Again, there is no wrong or right way to deal with this situation, but one thing is certain—something must be done in order to protect the teacher from liability. Alerting administration may be the best course of action, but for their own protection teachers must also document all actions that they take.

Taking the appropriate steps to protect teachers from liability is not a matter of self-interest. The protection of students is the most important goal. The fact is, these children are in the teacher's care for substantial periods of time and their well-being is the biggest priority for ensuring a safe learning environment. Legal guidelines are set for teachers to follow, and if disregarded, the students are protected by the right to be compensated for any wrongdoing (Sewall 1995). The tort laws are intended to protect the victims, but more and more in the teaching profession the lines between accident and tort are becoming less and less visible.

Teachers must be aware of their liabilities, but sometimes that just isn't enough. Insurance and support from unions are now a must for teachers. Unpredictable accidents and incidents occur often. For example, a physical education teacher sent a student back to the locker room before class was over because of misconduct in class (Hasenfus, 1999). The student returned to the locker room and proceeded to try to hang herself. Her unsuccessful suicide attempt left her with permanent injuries. These injuries, the parents claimed, were due to negligence on the part of the teacher. Three years after the incident, the parents sued. Because of the girl's background and many suicide attempts by other students in previous months, the parents claimed "negligent infliction of emotional disease" on the part of the town, the school board, the superintendent, the principal, and the P.E. teacher (Hasenfus, 1999). This suit is an example of negligence that is hard to prove, but teachers are increasingly becoming aware of their liability.

Another example of this type of case deals with a class of second graders. Their teacher took them on a field trip to the beach and gathered the class for a picture of everyone on a log. Unfortunately, a wave swept over the log while the class was posing and knocked students off, and the log rolled over on one student, causing a fracture to her skull. The parents of this student sued the teacher, claiming negligence for putting their child in danger (Zirkel, 1991). Injury to a student because of negligence has to be due to the teacher's unreasonable behavior. Although these cases are hard to prove on the parents' side, they can cost teachers thousands of dollars in legal fees, and often will put their jobs in jeopardy.

Even when the there is an injury due to a decision made on the teacher's part, the courts take into account the state of the student and the student's decision-making skills. On a field trip in 1986, an eighth grade student asked and was granted permission by the teacher to leave the group at a restaurant and cross the street to a park. While crossing the street, the student was hit by a car. These cases bring up some necessary concerns about liability that have caused some degree of fear for teachers in schools today.

Unions and insurance agencies are responding to this by offering close to one million dollars of coverage for teachers, on average. Jessica Portner, a writer in *Educator Week*, states that teachers will face an array of allegations, from failing to protect students from harm, to harming students with too-severe punishments. In order to combat these concerns, the National Education Association (NEA) and the American Federation of Teachers (AFT) have become the largest providers of insurance for teachers (Portner, 2000). They cover more than 80 percent of the teachers in the U.S. public school systems (Portner, 2000). The AFT surveyed its members' opinions of what was wanted from their union, and "occupational liability protection" was ranked in the top three (Portner, 2000). With the NEA's dues paid each year, teachers can draw up to one million dollars in case of civil suits (Portner, 2000). The union also offers up to twenty-five thousand dollars in criminal cases. Director of member advocacy, Lynn Ohman, argues for the importance of this coverage, and says, "[t]eachers are frequently falsely accused of abuse and assault, and that can ruin someone's career. Without this coverage, it is difficult for teachers to cover the bills of legal assistance and responsibilities" (Portner, 2000).

Rob Knowles, a teacher accused of abuse, said he would have never been able to afford the legal bills without the help of union insurance. The AFT and NEA pay for lawyers on the teacher's side during employment disputes. Although there are many teachers who agree with Knowles, one union president, John Cole, of the Texas Federation of Teachers, has another opinion. Cole claims that the increase in coverage "is an expenditure of money that does no good for anybody" (Portner, 2000). He says, "the dues should be spent on lobbying the legislature for better benefits." But, he admits, "it keeps unions in business with competition." Competition includes insurance companies who are also offering similar coverage for teachers on an individual basis.

The insurance agency, Forrest T. Jones & Company is one that offers up to one million dollars coverage, even for student teachers (Forrest, 2002). Listed as covered allegations are: (1) injuries to a student under your supervision; (2) improper placement of students; (3) improper methods employed in instruction, counseling, research design, etc.; (4) defamation; (5) failure to educate; (6) failure to promote students or grant credit; (7) violation of students' civil rights; (8) negative consequences in the implementation of recommendations of research studies (Forrest, 2002).

To receive this extra coverage, teachers or student teachers must be members of the company's sponsoring associations and/or be a licensed educator. This professional liability plan offers teachers and student teachers more security in the case of torts.

Leaders of unions have voiced their concerns about private insurers playing on the fears of the teachers and marketing insurance that teachers do not really need. They also claim that because of some state laws that guard teachers from lawsuits, teachers are unsure about what kind of coverage they need. Bidding wars and increased maximum awards have been the result of private insurance policies (Portner, 2000). Insurance protection is the umbrella, which buffers teachers from unfair liability cases as well as true accusations.

As educators in the United States, teachers are required to perform two specific tasks. First, teachers must provide instruction for their students regarding educational matters. Second, teachers must provide supervision for their students. Teachers must provide a safe learning environment in which the students will be protected from any form of harm. Providing a safe learning environment can be a difficult task for teachers because there are multiple situations in which their students may be in jeopardy. Teachers are required by law to be aware of their liability in the classroom. Ignorance of the law is no excuse.

The following are possible suggestions and tips a teacher in the public school system should be aware of to avoid a lawsuit: First year teachers are typically at a higher risk of being found "negligent" because they are not familiar with school policies and procedures. Vicki Petzko (1998), an Associate Professor of the Educational Administration and Supervision of the University of Tennessee states that a teacher's lack of knowledge, expertise, and/or experience can easily lead to legal trouble. She also notes that first year teachers are at an extremely high risk for being caught in a legal disaster. First year teachers must be cautious when they begin their career because they lack experience and knowledge about school policy. One suggestion Petzko mentions is that first year teachers must be willing to ask experienced teachers questions regarding their liability as a teacher. Experienced teachers are an excellent resource for understanding the process, rules, and procedures teachers must comply with in their respected school districts to avoid a lawsuit. In the *Larson v. Independent School District*, a first year teacher was found liable for the paralyzing of an eighth grade student, even though the teacher claimed he lacked experience in the activity in which the student was hurt (Cotton, 1995). The teacher's lack of experience is no excuse when a student's safety is in danger. Petzko (1998) also noted that first year teachers must be firmly aware of the state laws and school board policies regarding the use of force or physical punishment because these matters can often lead to lawsuits.

Teachers must have quality, effective communication lines with the administrators of their school districts. Administrators are another excellent resource for understanding the liability of a teacher. Some administrators are more familiar with the rules and regulations of a school than any other staff members of a school district. They are more aware of school district laws, as they have studied the law more extensively than any other staff member. Administrators should be the primary source for teachers to discuss legal matters with because one of the major roles of administrators is to prevent any legal issues from escalating into lawsuits.

Physical education teachers and coaches are typically the two most vulnerable positions in the public school. Vicki Petzko (1998) notes that 42 percent of negligent suits filed by students were filed against either coaches or physical education teachers. She also notes that over half of the injuries that occurred in schools were a result of participating in an after-school sport. Physical education classes and extracurricular activities require the student to be physically active. Coaches and physical educators must provide proper supervision, and there must be proper safety instructions prior to the given activity. Doyice Cotton (1995), a faculty member of the Department of Health Science and Physical Education at Georgia Southern University, states that physical education teachers should be liable for the accidents that occur in their classroom when a student teacher is working for them. It is their responsibility to educate any student teachers and take any responsibility for not providing a safe learning environment. In the case of *Brahatcek v. Millard School District*, (1979) a student was killed by another student, and the student teacher was found negligent because he was focusing on an individual student, not supervising the class as a whole (Cotten, 1995). Physical educators and coaches must also provide proper training for their assistants. If the proper training does not take place, the assistant should not be required to perform the assigned tasks because the risk of a lawsuit is too great. Physical educators and coaches must also remember to focus their attention on the entire class or team because teachers or coaches will be liable for any harm done to a student that could have been avoided if proper supervision had taken place.

Teachers must understand school policies regarding field trips, and students also must be aware of the rules and expectations the teacher and school require when traveling. Vicki Petzko (1998) notes that overnight field trips are a legal disaster waiting to occur if students are not aware of the off-campus school policy. Teachers must explain to the students what is expected of them on a field trip. Teachers must also know their own rights regarding the extent to which they can search students if they have brought something on the trip that is forbidden. If a student is injured or lost on a field trip, the teacher must know how to respond to the given situation. Science teachers and vocational teachers must be cautious when students are handling chemicals, tools, and are near possible trip hazards on the floor. Schools are required by law to properly assess possible risks of the school's activities in a common school day (Wenham, 1999). Teachers of vocational classes or science classes, where there might be a laboratory, are required to take into consideration any possible safety liability they may be held accountable for. If a teacher does not recognize a potential danger and a student gets injured, the teacher may be liable for the injury of the student. Whether the safety procedure is associated with the proper use of a power tool, or with a potential trip danger on the floor, teachers are required by law to provide a safe learning environment (Wenham, 1999). Teachers should ask other experienced vocational teachers about safety procedures, such as safety glasses, or about any other possible safety suggestions they may have to offer.

Teachers and students are exposed to many situations wherein careless negligence can occur. Children are prone to take risks, act carelessly, and ignore simple cautions. In matters of student supervision teachers cannot be too careful.

Glossary

LEGAL TERMS FOR TEACHERS

A

ACQUITTAL–A verdict or finding of not guilty by a jury or a judge in the case of a bench trial.

AFFIDAVIT–A written statement under oath declaring certain facts to be true.

ALLEGATION–The assertion of fact made in legal proceedings.

ANSWER–Defense in writing made by a defendant to the allegation contained in a bill, indictment, or complaint filed against him by a plaintiff.

APPEAL– An application or petition by an appellant to a higher administrative body or court to rectify the order of the administrative body or court below.

APPEARANCE–A coming into court as a party to a suit, whether as plaintiff or defendant.

APPELLANT–One who appeals from an administrative or a judicial decision.

APPELLATE COURT–A higher court which hears a case from a lower court on appeal.

APPELLEE–The person against whom an appeal is taken: the respondent to an appeal.

ARBITRARY–Means in an "arbitrary" manner, as fixed or done capriciously or at pleasure: not founded in the nature of things; non-rational; not done or acting according to reason or judgment; depending on the will alone; absolutely in power, capriciously; tyrannical; despotic.

ARRAIGNMENT–In criminal practice, to bring a prisoner to court to answer to a criminal charge after being advised of his constitutional rights.

ASSAULT–Threatening to strike or harm.

AT ISSUE–Whenever the parties to a suit come to a point in the pleadings that is affirmed on one side and denied on the other, they are said to be "at issue."

B

BAIL–The deposit of money with a court to permit the release of a person from legal custody. Return of the deposit is conditioned upon the person's appearance at the time and place designated.

BAR–Refers to attorneys, counselors, and advocates of the court collectively.

BATTERY–Beating and wounding, including touching or laying hold, however trifling, of another's person or clothes in an angry, insolent or hostile manner.

BENCH WARRANT–A court order directing that a defendant who had failed to appear for a scheduled court appearance be arrested and brought to court.

BILL OF INDICTMENT–A formal written document accusing a person of having committed a felony or misdemeanor, laid before a grand jury for their action upon it.

BOUNDOVER–The action whereby a lower court requires a person to appear for trial in a higher court after cause has been found.

BREACH–A breaking: either the invasion of a right or the violation of a duty.

BRIEF–The written document used by counsel to convey to the appellate court the essential factors of the client's case, a statement of the questions of law involved, the law he would have applied and the application he desires made of it by the court.

C

CASE LAW–Non-statutory law, based on past decisions, opinions, interpretations, and traditions.

CERTIORARI–(To be more fully informed) An original writ or action whereby a cause is removed from an inferior to a superior court for trial. The record of proceedings is then transmitted to the superior court. The term is most commonly used when requesting the U.S. Supreme Court to hear a case from a lower court.

CHARGE–(1) In criminal law, the accusation made against a person. (2) In civil and criminal law, it also refers to the instructions on law that the court gives the jury at the end of a trial.

CHIEF JUSTICE–The presiding judge of a court.

CIRCUIT–A division or territory for judicial business.

CIVIL ACTION–An action, which has for its object the recovery of private or civil rights, or compensation for their infraction.

CLASS BILL OR SUIT–One in which one or more members of a class sue either for themselves or for themselves and other members of a class.

CODE–A compilation of statutes, scientifically analyzed into chapters, subheadings, and sections with a table of contents and an index. A collection or system of laws.

COMMON LAW–Legal principles derived from usage and custom, or from court decisions affirming such usage and custom, or from the acts of Parliament in force at the time of the American Revolution, as distinguished from law created by enactment of American legislatures.

CONCURRING OPINION–An opinion, separate from that which embodies the views and decision of the majority of the court, prepared and filed by a judge who agrees with the general result of the decision, and which either reinforces the majority opinion by the expression of the particular judge's own views or reasoning, or (more commonly) voices his/her disapproval of the grounds of the decision or the arguments on which it was based, though approving the final result.

CONTEMPT–Willful disobedience of the order of a court or administrative tribunal.

CONTINUANCE–The postponement of a legal proceeding to another set date.

CONTRACT–A promissory agreement between two or more persons, groups or organizations that creates, modifies, or destroys a legal relation.

CONVICTION–The result of a criminal trial that ends in a judgment or sentence that the prisoner is guilty as charged.

COSTS–Monetary allowance made to the successful party from the losing party for his expenses in prosecuting or defending a suit.

COUNTERCLAIM–A claim presented by a defendant in opposition to the claim of the plaintiff.

COURT TERM–A division of the year during which the court holds its sessions.

CROSS-EXAMINATION–The questioning of the opponent's witness by a party or attorney.

D

DAMAGES–A pecuniary compensation of indemnity, which may be recovered in the courts by any person who has suffered loss, detriment, or injury, whether to his/her person, property, or rights through the unlawful act or omission or negligence of another.

DECREE–The judgment of a court of equity or admiralty answering for most purposes to the judgment of a court of common law.

DEFAMATION–Scandalous words written or spoken concerning another, tending to the injury of his/her reputation, for which an action on the case for damages would lie.

DEFENDANT–A person who is being sued in a civil action or is prosecuted in a criminal action.

DEPOSITION–A written statement made under oath taken outside of the court but to be used at trial.

DISCOVERY–A proceeding whereby one party to an action may be informed as to facts known by other parties or witnesses.

DISMISSAL–An order disposing of an action by sending it out of court without trial of the issues involved. A dismissal may bar a new suit on the same grounds (Dismissal with Prejudice) or may permit a new suit on the same grounds (Dismissal without Prejudice).

DISSENTING OPINION–An opinion disagreeing with that of the majority, handed down by one or more members of the court.

DOUBLE JEOPARDY–Charging an accused with a crime for which he has already been tried.

DUE PROCESS–Regular and orderly administration of justice by a court in accordance with established rules.

E

EN BANC–A judicial bench. The term is usually applied to a court of appeal when all of its judges sit together and jointly issue a decision or opinion.

ENJOIN–To require, command, positively direct. To require a person, by writ of injunction from a court of equity, to perform, or to abstain or desist from, some act.

EX POST FACTO–(After the fact) An act passed after another act, which retroactively changes the legal consequences of that act. Federal Constitution prohibits passage of ex post facto criminal law.

H

HEARSAY EVIDENCE–Evidence not proceeding from the personal knowledge of the witness, but from the mere repetition of what he/she has heard others say.

HEARING–Formal public proceeding with definite issue to be tried, in which parties proceeded against have a right to be heard.

I

IN LOCO PARENTIS–In place of the parent: charged with some of the parents' rights, duties, and responsibilities.

INDICTMENT–A formal accusation made by a grand jury charging a person with having committed a crime.

INJUNCTION–A prohibitive writ issued by a court of equity forbidding the defendant to do some act he/she is threatening, or forbidding him/her to continue doing some act which is injurious to the plaintiff and cannot be adequately redressed by law.

INTERROGATORIES–A series of written questions directed by one party to another, which seek out potential evidence and call for written answers.

J

JUDGMENT–The decision by a court upon respective rights of the parties in a civil case or the decision of the guilt or innocence of the accused in a criminal case.

JURISDICTION–The geographical area and the type of cases over which a court has authority.

JURY–A group of people sworn to hear the evidence and inquire into the facts in a law case, and to give a decision in accordance with their findings.

JUVENILE COURT–Court having jurisdiction over those young persons legally defined as juveniles.

L

LACHES–Negligence, or unreasonable delay in pursuing a legal remedy, whereby a person forfeits his/her right.

LIABILITY–The word is a broad legal term and has been referred to as the most comprehensive in significance, including almost every character of hazard or responsibility, absolute, contingent, or likely.

LIBEL–Defamation by printed or written communication.

M

MANDAMUS–A writ of mandamus is a command from a court of law directed to an inferior court, officer, corporate body, or person regarding him/her or them to do some particular thing.

N

NEGLIGENCE–Want of care.

O

ORIGINAL JURISDICTION–The authority of a court to hear cases of the first instance, as opposed to appellate jurisdiction.

P

PARTIES–The persons who take part in the prosecution or defense of any legal proceeding.

PER SE–By itself, alone.

PERJURY–The legal offense of testifying falsely and deliberately under oath.

PETITION–Written application or prayer to an administrative body or the court for the redress of a wrong or the grant of a privilege or license.

PLAINTIFF–Person who brings an action, one who sues by filing a complaint.

PLEADINGS–Successive statements by which litigants set forth the grounds upon which they base their own claims or challenge the claims of their opponents.

PRAYER–The request contained in a bill in equity that the court will grant the process, aid, or relief, which the complaint desires.

PRECEDENT–A decision considered as furnishing an example or authority for an identical or similar case afterward arising on a similar question of law.

PRELIMINARY HEARING–A hearing given a person charged with a crime by a magistrate or judge to determine whether he should stand trial.

PRETRIAL PROCEDURE–A device that consist of conferences between the attorneys for the parties to a lawsuit and a judge of the court. The chief purpose of this is to prepare the case for an effective trial by formulating the issues and stating them in a pretrial order that then, in effect, becomes the chart for the trial.

PRIMA FACIE–At first view, on the first aspect. Prima facie evidence, presumptions, etc., are such as will prevail, if not rebutted, or disproved.

PROBABLE CAUSE–An apparent state of facts found to exist in a criminal case that the accused person had committed the crime charged, or in a civil case, that a cause of action existed.

Q

QUASI–As if. Almost.

R

RATIFICATION–In a broad sense, the confirmation of a previous act done either by the party himself/herself or by another: confirmation of a voidable act.

REMAND A CASE–An action by an appellate court to send the case back to the court from which it came for further proceedings there.

REMEDY–The relief given by a court to secure to an injured party his rights.

RES JUDICATA–A matter judicially decided.

RESPONDENT–The one making an answer- the defendant.

RESTRAIN–To prohibit from acting to enjoin.

RESTRAINING ORDER–An injunction.

S

SERVICE–The delivery of a writ, notice, injunction, etc., officially notifying that person of some action or proceeding in which he/she is concerned.

SLANDER–Defamation by spoken word.

STARE DECISIS–Adherence to precedent. When the court has made a declaration of legal principle it is the law until changed by a competent authority.

STATUTE–Law enacted by the legislative power of a country or state.

STIPULATION–An agreement between the parties or their attorneys.

SUBPOENA–A court order requiring a witness to attend. It may also order him to bring books or records with him.

SUBSTANTIVE LAW–The positive law of right and duties.

SUMMARY JUDGMENT–A judgment on the basis of the pleadings and, if any, affidavits of the parties where there is no dispute regarding the facts material to the case.

SUMMONS–The process by which a defendant is advised that there is a claim against him or her. It may also be a notification to a witness or juror to appear in court.

SUPREME COURT–An appellate court: the court of last resort in the federal system and in most states.

T

TENURE–Right to perform duties and receive emoluments thereof.

TESTIMONY–Words heard from a witness in court, as distinguished from evidence derived from writings.

TORT–Legal injury or wrong committed upon the persons or property of another independent of contract.

TRANSCRIPTS–An official record of proceedings recorded by the court stenographer.

TRIAL–A proceeding in court where the charge and facts in question are viewed and the guilt or innocence of the defendant is determined.

TRIAL DE NOVO–A new trial or retrial in an appellate court in which the whole case is gone into as if no trial had been held in a lower court.

V

VERDICT–The formal decision or finding made by a jury.

VOID–Null; ineffectual; nugatory; having no legal force or binding effect; unable in law to support the purpose for which it was intended.

W

WAIVE–Voluntary surrender of a right, claim, or privilege

References

AAUP—1940 Statement of Principles on Academic Freedom and Tenure with 1970 Interpretive Comments. Retrieved February 12, 2004 from: http://www.aaup.org/statements/Redbook/1940stat.htm.

Areen, Judith. 1992. Cases and Materials on Family Law. New York. The Foundation Press, Inc.

Alexander, Kern and M. David. 1997. The Law of Schools, Students and Teachers. Minnesota. West Publishing.

Ayres, A. 1993. The wisdom of Martin Luther King, Jr. New York: Meridian.

Bias Incidents on Campus. [On-line]. Retrieved March 1, 2004 from: http://www.studentsforacademicfreedom.org/archive/december/biasincidents 120503.htm

Cauchon, D. April 13, 1999. Zero-tolerance policies lack flexibility. *USA Today,* p. 1-6.

Common School Manual of the State of Washington, 2003.

Cooper, W., & Terrill, T. 2002. The American South, A History: Connecticut. McGraw-Hill,

Cotten, Doyice J. 1995. Liability of Educators for the Negligence of Others: Substitutes Aides, Student Teachers, and New Teachers. *Physical Educator,* 52 n2, p. 70-77.

Cozzens, L. 1995. Brown v. Board of Education. May 6, 2004 from: http://www.watson.org/~lisa/blackhistory/early-civilrights/brown

Euben, D.R. May 2002. Academic Freedom of Individual Professors and Higher Education Institutions: The Current Legal Landscape. [On-line essay]. http://www.aaup.org/Com-a/aeuben.HTM.

Family Education Network. 2003. *Civil Rights Movement Timeline.* May 6, 2004, from http://www.infoplease.com/spot/civilrightstimeline1.html

Faraguna, R. & Garrett, V. 1993. *Basic Family Law.* Shepard's McGraw-Hill Pub. New York, New York.

First Amendment Schools. Retrieved February 14, 2004 from: http://www.firstamendmentschools.org/freedoms/faq.aspx?id=12820

Forrest T. J. & Co. January 2002. Professional liability protection plan for student. Retrieved February 16, 2004 from: ftj .com/2001 /TIE/student-teacher? proliability.

Hartin, E. R. 2003. *Plessy vs. Ferguson.* April 26, 2004, from http://campus.northpark.edu/history/WebChron/USA/PlessyFerguson.CP.html

Hasenfus v. LaJeunesse. 1999. *In Educational Law.* Retrieved March 10, 2004 from: www. web.lexis-nexis.com/universe/document.

Harvard Law School Forum. December 7, 1951. Can We Afford Academic Freedom? Retrieved February 12, 2004 from: http://www.law.harvard.edu/students/orgs/forum/Academic.html.

Hazard, William R. 1978. Education and the Law. The Free Press: division of Macmillan Publishing MN:

Heins, M. Spring 2001. Academic Freedom Bites the Dust. [On-line]. Retrieved March 10, 2004 from: http://www.ncac.org/cen news/cn81academic freedom.html

Goldstein. A. P., Apter, S. J., & Harootunian, B. 1984. School violence. Englewood Cliffs, New Jersey: Prentice-Hall.

Graves, B. 1994. When the abuser is an educator: Dealing with sex abuse. *Administrator.* 51. p. 8-20.

Johnson, Collins and Johansen D. 1991. *Foundations of American Education* Allyn and Bacon, Boston. p. 225.

Kasim, M. S. et.al. 1995. Childhood deaths from physical abuse. Child Abuse and Neglect: *The International Journal* 19, p. 847-854.

Katz, K.D. 1983. The First Amendment's Protection of Expressive Activity in the University Classroom: A Constitutional Myth. *University California Davis Law Review.* Vol. 16, p. 857-931.

Kopka, D. L. 1997. *School Violence.* Santa Barbara CA: Contemporary World Issues.

Kreklewetz, C. M. & Piotrowski, C. C. 1998. Incest survivor mothers: Protecting the next generation. Child Abuse and Neglect: *The International Journal.* 22. p. 1305- 1312.

La Morte, M. 1996. *School Law: Cases and Concepts.* Boston: Allyn and Bacon.

Lee P. Arbetman and others (1994). *Street Law: A Course in Practical Law*. West Publishing Company, MN.

Lichman, A. 2001. Zero tolerance policies in schools. [On-line]. Retrieved March 10, 2004 from: http ://ncnc. essortment. com/zerotolerancep raow.htm.

Loevy, R. D. 1997. *The Civil Rights Act of 1964: The Passage of the Law that Ended Racial Segregation*: New York Press.

Manchester, W. 1993. *A world lit only by fire: The medieval and the renaissance, portrait of an age*. Boston: Little, Brown and Company.

McAndrews, T. March 2001. Zero tolerance policies. [On-line]. Retrieved April 15, 2004 from: http://npin.org/library/2001/nO0540/nO0540.html.

McCarthy, M. Martha and Cambron, H. Nelda (1981). Public School Law: Teachers' and Students' Rights. Allyn & Bacon. pp. 307-8.

McCune, C. 2001. Schools'Zero Tolerance Policies: Effective Deterrent or Draconian Overreaction?. [On-line]. Retrieved April 15, 2004 from: http://www2.widener.edu/McCune.html.

New Jersey Department of Education. 2004. *Brown vs. Board of Education*. May 3, 2004, from http://www.njpep.org/tutorials/BrownvBoard/supreme courtcases.htm

Nolen, C. 2001. *African American Southerners in Slavery, Civil War and Reconstruction, Jefferson, North Carolina*: McFarland & Company, Inc.

Orfield, G., & Lee, C. 2004. *Brown at 50: King's Dream or Plessy's Nightmare?* April 22, 2004, from http://www.civilrightsproject.harvard.edu

Overbec, Wayne 1995. *Major Principles of Media Law*. For Worth: Harcourt Bruce, p. 450-464.

Peterson, J. Leroy, Rossmiller, H. Richard, & Marlin M. Voltz. 1978. *The Law and Public School Operation*. New York: Harper and Row. P.345.

Price, J.R., Levine, A.H., & Cary, E. (1988). The Rights of Students. Carbondale, IL: Southern Illinois Press.

Principal Strip Searches Student Suspected of Theft. *School Law Bulletin*. Quinlin Publishing Company, Boston, MA. Vol. 21, No. 2, Feb. 1994. p. 2.

Peters, R. DeV.; McMahon, R. J.; & Wolfe, D. A. 1997. *Child abuse: New directions in prevention and treatment across the lifespan*. Thousand Oaks, California: SAGE Publications, Inc.

Petzko, Vicki N. 1998. Preventing Legal headaches Through Staff Development: considerations and Recommendations. *NASSP Bulletin* v82, n602, p.35-42.

Portner, J. March 29, 2000. Fearful teachers buy liability insurance. *Education Week*. Retrieved January 23, 2002 from the World Wide Web: http://www.edweek.org.

Richey, C. A. & Whipple, E. E. 1997. Crossing the line from physical discipline to child abuse: How much is too much? Child Abuse & Neglect: *The International Journal.* 21. p. 431-444.

Sadker, Myra Pollack, and David Miller Sadker. 1997. Teachers, Schools, and Society. New York, McGraw-Hill, p. 360-361

Safe and Responsive Schools 2000. Zero tolerance. [On-line]. Available: http://www.indiana.edu/~safeschl/zero/html.

SAF: The Academic Bill of Rights. [On-line]. Retrieved February 12, 2004 from: http://www.studentsforacademicfreedom.org/abor.html.

Science Excellence for All Ohioans. [On-line]. Retrieved February 12, 2004 from: http://66.98.196.67/~balancedscience.net/sci1/reprints/ohio scientistslist.html

Sewall, Angela. Teacher liability: What we Don't Know Might Hurt Us. Retrieved April 12, 2004 from: http://www.auburn.edu/academic/education.

Shakeshaft, C. 1994. The use of background checks. *School Administrator,* 51. p. 24.

Smith, S.M. 1975. *The Battered Child Syndrome.* London: England Butterworth.

Standler, R.B. 1999. Academic Freedom in the USA. [On-line essay]. Retrieved February 9, 2004 from: http://www.rbs2.com/afree.htm.

Standler, R.B. 2000. Freedom of Speech in USA for Professors and Other Government Employees. [On-line essay]. Retrieved February 11, 2004 from: http://www.rbs2.com/afree.htm.

Stegmayer, W.J. 2000. Protecting Academic Freedom in the 21st Century. *Social Education.* 64(7), p. 422-426.

Strictness seems effective for zero tolerance policies in Georgia schools February 28, 1998. Athens Daily News [On-line]. Available: http://www.onlineathens.com/

Strope Jr., J.L. 1999. In our minds, the legal myth dies slowly! *National Association of Secondary School Principals. NASSP Bulletin,* 83(610), p. 14-22.

Tower, C.C. 1984. Child Abuse and Neglect: A teacher's handbook for detection reporting and classroom management. Washington, D.C.: *NEA* Professional Library, National Education Association.

U.S. Department of Education, National Center for Education Statistics 1997. Violence prevention. [On-line]. Available: http://nces.ed.gov/fastfacts/display.asp?id=54.

Valente, W.D., Valente, C.M. (1998). *Law in the Schools.* Upper Saddle River, NJ: Prentice-Hall.

Verger, J. 2001. The birth of academic freedom. *The Unesco Courier*, 54(11), p. 18.

Vital Issues of the Constitution 1971. Houghton Mifflin Company, Boston.

Wenham, David. 1999. Civil liability of Schools. Teachers and Pupils for Careless Behavior. London: SAGE, 365-374.

Wilson, J.K. The State of Academic Freedom, 2001-2002: A Report. [On-line]. Retrieved April 11, 2004 from: http://www.collegefreedom.org/report2002.htm.

Yell, Mitchell L. February 16, 1999. Tort Laws and Negligence for Special Education Students. Retrieved April 6, 2004 from: http://cecp.air.org/interact/authoronline.

Yudof, Mark. 1992. *Educational Policy and the Law.* St. Paul: West Publishing. CO.

Zirkel, P. May 1991. Staying out of court. Teacher Magazine. Retrieved January 23, 2002 from the World Wide Web: http://www.edweek.org

Zero tolerance nightmares 2001. [On-line]. Retrieved April 12, 2004 from: http://www.ztnightmares.com.